PERF

Is the best

Politics

How to create
high-performance government
using Lean Six Sigma

Graham Richard

Mayor, Fort Wayne, Indiana
2001-2007

ACKNOWLEDGEMENTS

I would like to acknowledge the following thought leaders who inspired me to apply new ideas and business practices in city government: Larry Bossidy, Jim Collins, W. Edwards Deming, Peter Drucker, Dot Feldman, Thomas Friedman, Mike George, Mikel Harry, Ron Hiefetz, Howard Gardner, Peter Kline, Peter Senge, and Jack Welch.

I'd also like to thank the following people for their ideas, support, and encouragement: my wife Mary Richard, Joy Hudson, Ryan Chasey, Scott Lasater, Dale Siegelin, Bruce Katz, Al From, Bill Buddinger, Senator Evan Bayh, and Governor Tom Vilsack.

Thanks to Ryan Chasey and Lindsey Maksim, who helped make this book a reality, to Joe Kimmell for his legal advice, and to Nelson Coats for financial advice. We also greatly appreciate the efforts of our production team: Sue Reynard, editor; proofers Brenda Quinn and Bonnie Blackburn, and photographer and cover designer Phil Hudson.

Finally, many thanks to the dozens of city employees who shared their stories and insights; you'll find their names and contributions to high-performance government throughout the book.

ISBN-13: 978-0-9791163-0-8

ISBN-10: 0-9791163-0-9

Contents

PREFACE

This book is for readers searching for best business practices to produce high-performance government. I believe in the great talent and boundless energy of the thousands of government employees and leaders who work hard to deliver the best services. In every city, town, and county and in every school district, leaders are seeking new ways to deliver better services.

Noted consultant and author Michael George heard about our effort to use Lean Six Sigma in city government and came to visit us in 2002. His subsequent book, *Lean Six Sigma for Service* (McGraw-Hill, 2003), features stories from organizations that demonstrated innovative uses of quality methods in services: Lockheed-Martin, Bank One, Stanford University Hospital, and the City of Fort Wayne, Indiana. Perhaps he captures the spirit of what we're doing with this paragraph from the introduction to his book:

> *"All of these people and their organizations were impressive, but it's the City of Fort Wayne, Indiana, that really amazed me—perhaps because I, like most people, had low expectations when it came to government services of any sort. What's really intriguing are the dozens of city employees who are reducing lead times, streamlining processes, providing better quality services to citizens, and holding down costs."*

This book continues the story of the hundreds of Fort Wayne city employees pursuing excellence in city services.

Graham Richard, November 2006

Chapter 1

Performance
and
Politics

In 2000, a citizen of Fort Wayne who called in a complaint about a pothole could have expected to wait two days before it was fixed. Jump forward five years to Spring 2005. An email from a resident says he called in a pothole before he left for a quick shopping trip and he saw the crew was already working on it when he got back.

Now, in 2008, the average time to fill a pothole after getting a call from a Fort Wayne citizen is 1.5 *hours*.

That's Performance.

Back again to 2000. If you had talked to anyone—a local business owner, a citizen—who had to deal with Fort Wayne city government, you'd likely have heard a lot of negative comments. The kindest of them would have fallen along the lines of "I hate it" and "It's a real hassle."

Talk to anyone today and you'll likely get a much different reaction. Projects like the one we did on land improvement building permits slashed the average turnaround time from 51 days to less than 9 days have led to very different perceptions of Fort Wayne government. One businessman stood up at a local builders' conference and said, "I used to hate doing business with the city. Now I get the permits I need much faster, hassle free."

That's Performance.

Back to 2000. The city faced a challenge as the recession began to hit. But even so, by January 1, 2003, we had built a cash safety net of over $23 million—thanks in large part to gains from projects like our street light inventory reduction effort, which has saved almost $600,000 to date. Total savings and cost avoidance from our Six Sigma and Lean efforts are currently running over $13.5 million.

That's Performance.

Travel back to November 1999. I won my first mayoral election by a mere 76 votes (out of more than 42,000 cast), an outcome that was subject to a recount and lawsuit. When I ran for re-election in 2003, I won by more than 7,500 votes (with a total of 58% of the vote).

That's the Politics of Performance.

Winning that 2003 election by such a large margin was a recognition of important changes that began in Fort Wayne city government in 2000. A lot of city employees worked very hard to learn new ways to conduct business. They're now using their new tools and skills to improve services for our citizens, and to make the city a safer, better place to live and work. Plus we've been able to lower the tax rate (see Figure 1, next page).

Figure 1:
Lowest Tax Rates Since the Late 1960s

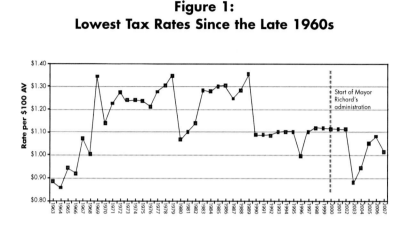

Here's another link between performance and politics. The gains we've made in recent years have allowed us to hold tax rates down despite an increase in population and demand for services. As you can see, we had some of the lowest tax rates since the late 1960s.

Becoming a Competitive City

Achieving election-winning government performance begins when city leaders and the mayor work together to create a competitive strategy.

The word "competitive" may sound out of place to some readers when used in reference to a city. After all, unlike private-sector businesses, governments have a guaranteed and relatively steady "customer" base that generates a reliable income stream from taxes and fees. But cities are very much in a competition when it comes to attracting new businesses, high-quality workers, new residents, and civic investments.

You don't have to be a mayor to know that the pressure on cities to perform is greater than ever. People know that jobs are scarce, that disaster preparations have a much higher priority after 9/11 and Hurricane Katrina, and that money is tight.

To make matters more challenging, Fort Wayne has recently gone through a series of annexations that has increased our population by about 15% (see Figure 2).

Figure 2:
Fort Wayne's Population vs.
Number of City Employees

Operational improvements have helped the city maintain a near-constant workforce level despite a drastic rise in population due to annexation.

So the question indeed is what can we do to make our cities more competitive? Creating city operations that rival the most efficient businesses in the world and make it easier for people to do business is not rocket science. That's not to say the changes will come easily. But it can be done. It all starts with a solid strategy.

> "Change is necessary. The key is being able to adapt to that change and improve at the same time."
>
> Matthew Wirtz,
> Assistant Manager of Planning and Design Services

Strategy Means Knowing Which Wind is Favorable

There's an old saying I find myself repeating frequently: if you don't know to which port you are sailing, no wind is favorable.

That's why the first and perhaps most difficult job of the Mayor is to pick the port. The projects we pursued, the methods we chose, the internal development efforts we undertook—all came about because they fit into three strategic priorities that I set in January 2000:

- **Safe City**: Become the safest city of our size
- **Quality Jobs**: Retain and gain quality jobs for our employees and citizens
- **B.E.S.T.**: Building Excellent Services with Teams

This book focuses on the changes we're making internally to improve how—and how well—we do our work. I want to share with you what we have learned on our journey.

The examples and cases you'll read about fall into three general streams of activity:

- Developing an appreciation for operational excellence
- Tapping into leadership potential
- Using teams and the most effective improvement tools available to tackle priority problems

Why these three particular paths? I'll let three stories explain why.

Excellence, not just improvement

The word "excellent" in the third strategic focus was a deliberate choice. Many people equate disciplines like Six Sigma with a need to "improve." I think you'll agree that urging city employees to "improve a little" is quite different from saying that we have to "achieve excellence." The latter creates the energy and urgency needed to build the imperative for Lean and Six Sigma efforts. We can "improve" simply by doing a better job at what we already do. But we can never achieve excellence unless we start to think and act in new ways. You can't make it OK for people to be satisfied with marginal progress. You must strive to be the best.

Why operational excellence matters

Early in my administration, I asked for a complete, detailed list of properties owned or leased by the city. I was told that such a list didn't exist. The businessman in me was appalled: how could you effectively manage all your resources and obligations if you didn't even know what they were?

About the same time, I spent weeks personally visiting every city department, asking a few simple questions such as "Who is your customer?" People would look at me like, "Well, I don't have any customers. I work for the city." Then I'd ask, "Are you getting better at doing your job?" And people would say, "Well, yeah! Of course I'm getting better!" I would then ask, "How do you know that? How do you measure progress?" Few could answer.

From these kinds of interactions I came to realize that there was no basic business focus in city government. Until people appreciated the need to control processes and the need to know *why* they were performing certain tasks, they would never see the need to improve or achieve excellence.

Tapping into the leadership potential in city employees

I think we all know that there is a certain stereotype of government employees, characterized by the dismissive comment, "It's good enough for government." Though layoffs aren't unheard of in city and state governments, the perception is that people take government jobs for the security. The theory is that if you believe you can't be fired, you have less motivation to work hard, let alone take initiative or make improvements—so your mindset becomes keeping your head down, taking no risks, just getting by, waiting out this mayor, maintaining the status quo.

In my experience, that's one stereotype that couldn't be further from the truth.

Almost every Fort Wayne city employee who was offered the chance to learn something new and to improve their leadership skills seized the opportunity—even though it often meant a lot of extra work in off-hours. Michele Hill, our first Black Belt and Quality Manager, tells me that she didn't really think she was qualified for those positions in the beginning. But she was more than willing to try. And her role in helping shape the first five years of our effort is undeniable.

Joe Johnson was a union worker in our sewer utility department for 13 years. When he learned that he could take the Six Sigma program, he jumped at the chance. "I always wanted to develop and get better," he says. "And I always advise people that if you have the opportunity to learn, take it." (See sidebar on next page.)

Bob Kennedy was in the fourth wave of Black Belt training and led the pothole project you'll read about on p. 29. He recalls putting in a lot of time outside of work to complete that project. "With our process," he says, "you definitely have to be dedicated to learning new skills."

Do these sound like people who are satisfied with just getting by in their jobs? Who are happy with the status quo? Who are afraid to put themselves forward? Definitely not. And they are just the tip of the leadership iceberg we've uncovered within our ranks (see Chapter 4 for more). They are the cornerstone of the **4Ts** that I often cite as critical for improvement: you already have the **talent** in your city.

What you need to add is **training, technology,** and **tools** to support that talent to its fullest extent.

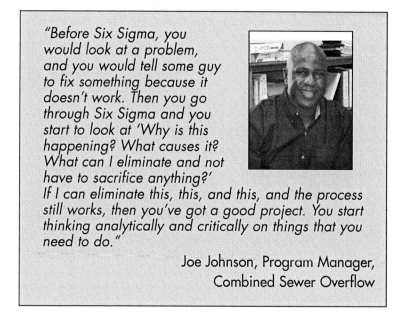

"Before Six Sigma, you would look at a problem, and you would tell some guy to fix something because it doesn't work. Then you go through Six Sigma and you start to look at 'Why is this happening? What causes it? What can I eliminate and not have to sacrifice anything?' If I can eliminate this, this, and this, and the process still works, then you've got a good project. You start thinking analytically and critically on things that you need to do."

Joe Johnson, Program Manager,
Combined Sewer Overflow

Lean Six Sigma: The most effective problem-solving method available

I knew from the moment I was elected that Six Sigma would play a big role in Fort Wayne's ability to achieve excellence. I'd been involved with quality improvement for decades. I was a founder of the Total Quality Management (TQM) Network in the Fort Wayne area in 1991. The early quality initiatives evolved into the field known as Six Sigma in the early 1990s, which has now morphed again to Lean Six Sigma.

The term "sigma" is taken from a Greek symbol that's used in statistics to represent variation in a measure. Achieving a "six sigma" level of quality means you have very little variation in a process, achieving a 99.9997% accuracy rate (fewer than 1 mistake in 300,000 tries). Few companies have achieved that level of quality in their processes, but many are getting closer every day. Six Sigma provides the tools and mechanisms to continuously improve quality by using a team-based structured problem-solving process that leads people from understanding customer needs to using data to analyze causes of problems and find solutions. But Six Sigma is more than just tools. The discipline emphasizes the need to develop a cadre of internal resources (with names like Black Belts, Green Belts, and Champions) who are trained in problem-solving, data analysis, and team and leadership skills.

The word "Lean" is the American term for a discipline that originated as the Toyota Production System. It's a set of tools that focus on process speed—primarily by eliminating waste and removing the causes of inefficiency.

Still, I rarely used the terms Six Sigma or Lean during my first campaign, for several reasons:

- Few citizens or employees knew what they meant
- The goal wasn't to use Six Sigma; it was to establish a city government that operated as effectively as any world-class company
- There are a lot of other aspects to improving how we do business as a city, and we would have lost the bigger picture had we focused attention only on Six Sigma or Lean

Focusing on the *purpose* of using Lean Six Sigma accomplishes several goals: It provides a rallying cry that is easier for people to get behind ("we want to be excellent" vs. "we want to use Lean Six Sigma") and encourages people to think about all the ways in which government operations can improve, not just focus on problems best solved through Lean Six Sigma.

Achievements

By the end of 2007, we had launched 131 Six Sigma projects (38 Black Belt and 93 Green Belt) and a 74 Lean projects, the vast majority of which had successful conclusions. Overall, we couldn't be prouder of the results. Specific successes include:

1. Getting better at what cities do

- We have improved a wide range of services (becoming faster at repairing potholes, issuing permits, and responding to incoming calls, for example; fewer pollutants in treated waste water; see Figure 3, next page)

Figure 3:
Sustained Reduction in Time to Repair Potholes

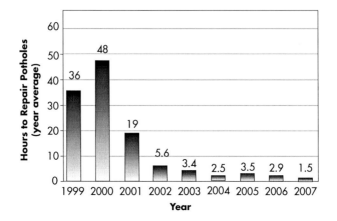

- We are now savvier consumers (our water utility staff, for example, is now famous for asking vendors for data that proves new equipment can perform at the required capability levels)

- We have improved safety for citizens and for city employees (see, for example, Figure 4, which shows how many fewer days are lost to accidents)

Figure 4:
Drop in Lost Days Due to Accidents

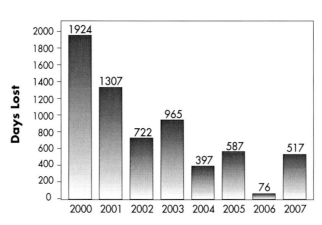

2. Realizing significant savings and cost avoidance (money freed up to be allocated for better or more services elsewhere)

- Various projects at our water pollution control and filtration plant have resulted in well over $150,000 saved

- Revised policies on non-public-safety take-home cars have saved $652,000 (from Lean Six Sigma and other changes)

- Reduced street light inventory has already saved $500,000 and more is to come (Figure 5)

Figure 5:
Street Light Inventory Savings

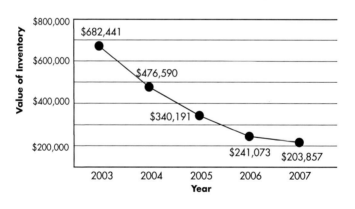

- Improvements in water filtration processes let us avoid repairs to a huge centrifuge (which minimally has delayed what will be a $1.7 million purchase— likely required at a later date, but we can determine when and plan accordingly); other improvements include reducing pollutants entering our waterways (Figure 6, next page)

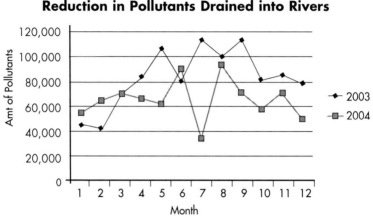

Figure 6:
Reduction in Pollutants Drained into Rivers

Operational improvements linked to Six Sigma projects have led to an annual cost savings of $280,000 at the water treatment plant and more than 100 fewer tons of pollutants draining into our rivers.

3. Eliminating process waste (which improves speed and reduces cost)

Every municipality has claims filed against it. "The fact is that most of these claims will not be paid due to protections provided by law," explains Mary Nelson-Janisse, our former risk manager (she has since been hired by a Fortune 100 company). "Still, every claim has to be reviewed." When she came on board in 2000, the average time to respond to a claim was 118 days, she recalls, and some claims stayed open twice as long. Everybody was unhappy—citizens, the insurance companies, the city. "I knew intuitively that the more time a claim is open, the more it costs you," says Mary. She led a project to study the process and discovered that the long claim review process was a result of having too many people involved. "We streamlined the reviews and now most claims are closed within a month," she says.

The rest of the story

Fast resolution also makes a big difference at a human level. "If I can respond to someone quickly, even if it's to say that their claim is not going to be paid—they may not be happy, but they are satisfied the claim has been handled. If I wait six months to a year or longer and then say no, they get very angry," explains Mary Nelson-Janisse. "They're also more likely to file in small claims court, but always lose, which leaves everyone unhappy."

Projects that work on streamlining work and eliminating waste are also part of our Lean efforts (see Chapter 5). As you can see in Figure 7, the savings and cost avoidance from just the efforts in our Public Works and City Utilities departments has totalled about $2.7 million through 2006.

Figure 7: Savings from Lean Projects

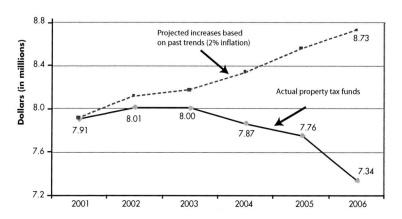

Lessons Learned #1

As pioneers in the application of Six Sigma and Lean inside city government, we've learned a lot about what works well and what doesn't. Some of the key lessons appear at the end of most chapters in hopes of shortening the learning curve in other cities. To start the list, here's one of the big lessons:

We should have better communicated our efforts and successes within and beyond government walls

As the old saying goes, it's not bragging if you perform. So I don't feel that I'm bragging when I say we have some great numbers and stories to share. But too few people in Fort Wayne know that. We have taken some steps—such as holding public celebrations of Lean and Six Sigma projects involving both the public and private sectors, and printing a portfolio of project summaries from our Public Works and City Utilities department.

"When you work for the Water Filtration Plant and you produce drinking water for 250,000 people, and you know that if you don't do it right people will get hurt—that's a serious burden on people. And they want to do it right. I think Lean Six Sigma gives them another tool to do it right."

Greg Meszaros
Director, Public Works and
City Utilities

But a lot of our employees, citizens, and other customers still don't understand what Lean Six Sigma is and what it's enabling us to do. That tells me we should have done more to communicate our involvement.

In particular, we didn't do enough, soon enough, to reach two critical audiences: city managers and the city council. Demonstrating that Lean Six Sigma is widespread in the business world—and not just some crazy whim of a new Democrat mayor—might have helped convince city employees and the Republican leaders on the city council that Lean Six Sigma is a valuable thing to do. And being able to demonstrate how we are using Lean Six Sigma to improve services and control costs can be used as leverage in keeping old businesses and attracting new ones. At one public meeting, a manager from the local Raytheon facility really got excited when he saw that city employees "could speak Six Sigma." To him, it was evidence that the city was serious about improvement and service.

Conclusion: "Can my city do this?"

Fort Wayne is a city of ordinary, hard-working people who have learned to do extraordinary things using a few simple principles and tools that radically changed their thinking about the best way to run a city government. The one factor that will determine whether you can do this in your city isn't what's happening there *now*. It isn't the background or education or even attitudes of city employees. It is not the current state of your budget. It is the determination of your leadership—and especially the mayor—to give people opportunities to work in new and better ways.

That word "opportunities" is critical in government environments. As Mayor, I don't have either the hire-and-fire authority or the flexible budgeting power that a corporate CEO has. So my ability to win through intimidation and incentives is limited. But my ability to win through opportunity creation is endless.

As a consequence, we have placed very few *demands* on city employees with regard to our Lean and Six Sigma efforts. Instead, we have focused on opening new doors to personal and professional growth, and many people have stepped through those doors willingly. They got to experience firsthand what Six Sigma and Lean have to offer, and develop new leadership skills they can use in their professional and personal lives.

A gratifying number of these people have become ambassadors for change and improvement—not by spouting any rhetoric they may have heard from me, but by sharing their own personal stories. For example:

"The Mayor never imposed learning, but he did create opportunities for it," recalls Paul Spoelhof, a senior

planner in our community development office. *"He told me, 'I want you to think of yourself as a civic entrepreneur.' At first, that didn't make sense to me. It sounded like just another buzzword. But now I see it means that if I keep learning and promoting learning, innovation will happen. People will have good ideas, and the best ones and most effective ones will eventually gain purchase and improve the organization and what we do."*

"I got myself noticed by applying for the superintendent job at the water filtration plant," says Vicky Zehr, who was an analytical chemist at the time. "I didn't get the job, but I was asked to participate in Six Sigma training shortly after the interview. I didn't know anything about the training, but I figured if they  were going to offer me some free education, I'd take it. The statistics were intimidating at first, but once I started the class, I realized that they weren't really that difficult. Additionally, I couldn't believe how beneficial statistics could be in my line of work." Vicky has applied what she learned in training to her routine work day. Now the Water Quality Supervisor, she evaluates data every day. "Six Sigma has made me more confident in the decisions I make as a manager," she says. "If I want to purchase a piece of equipment, I always get a demo piece, then utilize the Six Sigma tools to evaluate whether the equipment performs exactly the way the vendor claims it will. If it doesn't, I simply do not purchase the equipment. If it does, I will purchase the equipment and monitor its performance regularly utilizing the Six Sigma tools. This allows me to hold our vendors accountable using a credible data analysis process."

"When I came to work for the city in 2000, I didn't have a long-term vision of staying here. I thought the opportunities would be elsewhere," says Matthew Wirtz, our recently promoted Assistant Manager of Planning and Design Services in Public Works. "I thought the roles would be more prescriptive than in *the private sector. But now my perspective has been reversed. Working for this city, I've definitely been given opportunities to do a lot of different things that I wouldn't have gotten elsewhere. There's also an appreciation for people that's important to me."*

It is the achievements of people like these that has made our effort the success that it is. We here in Fort Wayne have demonstrated that it can work. And we hope that you can learn from our experience and make the same kinds of changes happen in your city.

Featured Project #1

Reducing Missed Garbage Pickups

Strangely enough, there are only a few processes where immediate feedback is guaranteed when a problem appears. Payroll is one of them: make a mistake on someone's paycheck and you'll hear about it immediately. Garbage pickups and filling potholes are two such processes for the city. They're highly visible, everybody cares about them, and you won't be kept in the dark for long if you're doing a lousy job at them. For those reasons, those two areas were chosen for some early Black Belt projects. Here is the first of these two projects.

As you read through this case, you may identify with the project leader's discovery that the city was "data rich but information poor." There is a lot of data generated by everyday city activities, but little of it is useful for improvement purposes. One of the secrets of Lean Six Sigma is that, often for the first time ever, people look at the right kind of data that tells them how their processes are performing, which in turn leads to improvement insights.

"Bob Young, who is the director of municipal services for our outside contractor for garbage pickup, told me that in 24 years in the business, he'd never had such a good relationship with any city," says Dawn Ritchie, the solid waste manager who led the project on missed garbage pickups as part of her Black Belt certification. "I know the staff at National Serv-All got really frustrated at times with how much effort was needed for the project," she adds, "but they stuck with it. And through all the data collection, surveys, and brainstorming, our relationship really blossomed."

Background

In Spring 2001, Dawn joined the second wave of Black Belt training (she later became just the fifth public official in the United States to be a certified Black Belt). Her supervisor suggested she tackle the problem of missed garbage pickups for her project.

Like many cities, Fort Wayne contracts out its garbage pickup, using a company called National Serv-All (NSA), which is a division of the more-famous Republic Services, the third-largest provider of environmental services in the country. To have any hope of making progress, the team had to include representatives of both the city and NSA. "We ended up with a five-person team," says Dawn. "Two from the city and three from NSA."

She adds that it wasn't hard to get NSA on board. "After all, each missed pick-up was costing them about $80." And when you consider there were nearly 4,900 misses per year, that added up to over $390,000. "Our initial goal was to cut that in half—get down to less than 2,500 misses a year," says Dawn. "That would save them more than $195,000 a year, or nearly a million dollars over the five-year contract."

Reducing missed garbage pickups required a collaboration between Fort Wayne's Dawn Ritchie and National Serv-All, the contractor, represented here by Ron Harmann (by truck).

Team

Dawn Ritchie - Black Belt Trainee
Ted Rhinehart - Champion
Matt Gratz, City Solid Waste
Angela Lewis, NSA Customer Service
Bob Young, NSA Municipal Services Mgr.
Mike Welch, NSA Operations

The Investigation

One step the team took was to gather data on what was actually happening. For a month, each customer service representative at NSA filled out a short questionnaire when a customer called about a missed pickup. The route supervisor, Mike Welch, filled out another questionnaire about the conditions at the time of the miss—the driver's experience, weather conditions, and so on.

Many of the results were predictable: Tuesday, the day with the heaviest schedule, also had the most misses. Trucks with temporary helpers had far more misses than those with regular staff. Drivers who had been on the job longer had far fewer misses than new employees.

A key step in the project was when the team performed what's known as an FMEA, a Failure Modes and Effects Analysis. FMEA is mostly used as an error-prevention tool, because it helps a team identify which types of errors are mostly likely to occur and cause serious problems—then come up with actions to prevent or counteract those errors. That way a team is focusing its attention on steps that will have the biggest impact on the problem.

Through FMEA, the team identified four areas they would concentrate on:

- Drivers being in a hurry
- Fatigued workers
- Turnover of workers
- Lack of communication

Solutions & Results

The team came up with a list of 15 specific recommendations linked to the areas of concentration, of which 13 were eventually implemented. Key changes included:

- Reducing the route size. This was accomplished in part by targeting some longer routes as "splitter routes" during the heaviest trash months of May/June and Sept/Oct—during those periods, a route that a driver could normally complete in 8 to 10 hours might take 14 hours or more. Select segments of these routes could be handed off to backup drivers during those heavy months.

- Changing the incentives so *speed* wouldn't be rewarded as much as *completeness*. This involved creating teams of five drivers who would receive extra pay if the team as a whole had fewer than 15 misses a week.

- Providing additional training.

- Increasing the number of helpers.

- Adding benefits to help with worker retention.

- Improving communication. Locations of frequent misses were marked on the map, there were more regular meetings with drivers and better mechanisms for driver feedback.

- Improving preventive maintenance.

- Increasing performance monitoring.

Though implementing these changes required extra dollars up-front, they ultimately led to more efficient services (and lower overall costs) as seen in the results.

Results

By the end of the project, missed trash pickups had dropped from an average of 94 per week to fewer than 47. (See Figure 8, next page.)

Figure 8: Missed Garbage Pickups

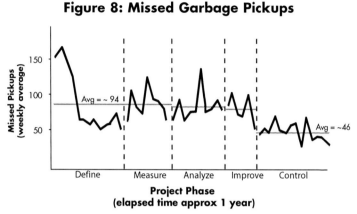

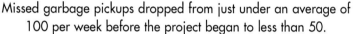

Missed garbage pickups dropped from just under an average of 100 per week before the project began to less than 50.

The savings estimate at the beginning of the project became a reality, with nearly $200,000 saved per year.

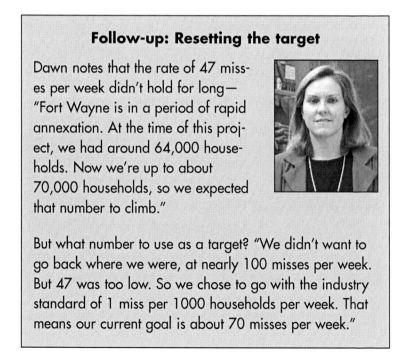

Follow-up: Resetting the target

Dawn notes that the rate of 47 misses per week didn't hold for long— "Fort Wayne is in a period of rapid annexation. At the time of this project, we had around 64,000 households. Now we're up to about 70,000 households, so we expected that number to climb."

But what number to use as a target? "We didn't want to go back where we were, at nearly 100 misses per week. But 47 was too low. So we chose to go with the industry standard of 1 miss per 1000 households per week. That means our current goal is about 70 misses per week."

What Made This Work

- Cooperative attitude: "There was tremendous cooperation by everyone involved," says Dawn. "Six Sigma brought the two sides together and strengthened the partnership, resulting in a lot more trust. New management out there is good, too."

She adds, "Driving down the number of misses was a great outcome but maybe the best thing to come out of this is the stronger relationship we have with the contractor. We now understand better where each other is coming from. That wasn't always the case. We learned so much about what Republic Services (NSA) was doing that we understood the process better. And that made us as city employees more effective."

Featured Project #2

Pothole Repair

Most cold-weather states take potholes seriously. They are not only a public safety issue but also a drain on public coffers; damage claims cost us nearly $7,600 the first quarter of 2001 alone (this project began in August of that year). Bob Kennedy was an ideal person to lead this project. A self-proclaimed "data person," he (like all of our Black Belts) put in a lot of extra time crunching these numbers and going where the data led him, encountering a few surprises along the way.

"I thought originally that if we could get the cycle time down to 12 hours [from 2 days], we'd be doing great," says Bob Kennedy, now the Associate Director of Public Works and City Utilities. "We've been under 3 hours for more than three years, and in 2007 had an average repair time of 1.5 hours, which is amazing. Once you get the initial improvements, maintaining them is the key to getting real payback."

Background

Some city services are seen by only a small fraction of the population. Others, like pothole repair, are seen by everybody—residents, workers, visitors. Northern drivers know well that the freeze-thaw cycles of winter and early spring can make huge potholes appear seemingly overnight. Historically, pothole repair has also caused huge overtime expenses, draining city resources.

Employees of the Fort Wayne Street Department know that street repair and maintenance had suffered in the late 1990s. The result was a large and growing number of complaints—and increasing damage claims against the city. When the opportunity to tackle the problem came up in conjunction with Black Belt training, Bob Kennedy jumped at the chance.

Team
Brad Baumgartner, Jill Morgan, Brooks Beatty
Bob Kennedy (Black Belt)
Ted Rhinehart (Champion)

The Investigation

The first question for most teams is "just how bad is the problem?" Answering that question takes data. Not surprisingly, Bob discovered that nobody was really tracking the data, although the pertinent facts were logged. "The operators would log the time that each complaint was received," he explains, "and the crews would log when the job was complete. But that data simply wasn't being used originally."

So the first step was combing through past records to compile the needed data. What Bob discovered was that the team was meeting the goal of repairing potholes within 24 hours only 77% of the time.

Overall numbers are great to use as a gauge, but they provide few clues for improvement. So Bob's team took a more detailed look at the data by creating the dot plot in Figure 9. The average repair time during the period studied was around 21 hours, but as you can see, many repairs took much longer to complete, trailing out for days.

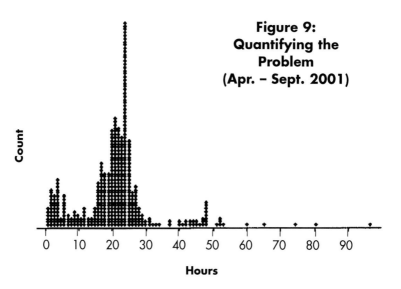

**Figure 9:
Quantifying the
Problem
(Apr. – Sept. 2001)**

Count

Hours

Each dot represents the time it took to complete one repair. The plot shows a pattern typical of time measurements: there is more than just one peak and the points trail out one end. This pattern is common because some types of jobs go very quickly (the small peak toward the left), the majority of work centers around an average (the largest peak), and a few jobs that, for whatever reason, take a long time to complete. The tallest spike is also typical of time measurements when people are pushing to meet a goal (here, it was to fill potholes within 24 hours).

The team also mapped out the process (a portion of which is shown in Figure 10), then brainstormed ideas about possible causes of problems.

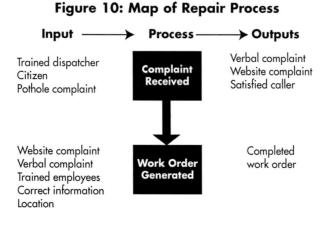

Figure 10: Map of Repair Process

Input ⟶ Process ⟶ Outputs

Trained dispatcher
Citizen
Pothole complaint

Complaint Received

Verbal complaint
Website complaint
Satisfied caller

Website complaint
Verbal complaint
Trained employees
Correct information
Location

Work Order Generated

Completed
work order

This kind of process map, called a SIPOC diagram (for Supplier-Input-Process-Output-Customer) succinctly captures the essential elements of a process.

Going into the project, the team was sure that potholes were worst in the southeast (SE) quadrant of town. And they felt there were likely differences in how pothole repair was handled in each quadrant that contributed to the problem. Were these preconceived notions correct? The first eye-opener for them was the data shown in Figure 11. Contrary to popular belief, the northeast quadrant had the largest number of potholes reported, even more than the southeast quadrant.

Figure 11: Pothole Complaints by Quadrant

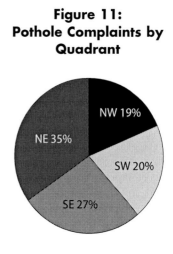

NW 19%
NE 35%
SW 20%
SE 27%

Surprise #2: not only did the SE quadrant have far fewer pothole problems than supposed, the average repair time in the SW was significantly faster than in other quadrants (see Figure 12).

Figure 12: Average Repair Time by Quadrant

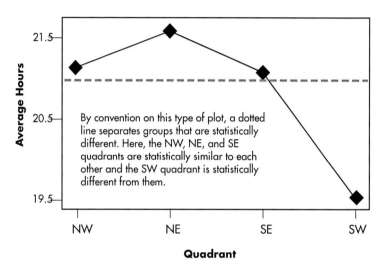

By convention on this type of plot, a dotted line separates groups that are statistically different. Here, the NW, NE, and SE quadrants are statistically similar to each other and the SW quadrant is statistically different from them.

This diagram shows the average pothole repair time for each quadrant (lower numbers mean faster service). Statistical tests showed that that SW quadrant was significantly faster than the other three.

The obvious question is what's happening in the SW quadrant that's different from the other three. The answer? Says Bob, "We talked to all the supervisors and found that the SW supervisor stopped by the dispatch office at noon each day—in addition to the usual morning pickup—to get new orders out to the crew. The others just picked up complaints once a day in the morning. That one step, which none of the other supervisors did, saved almost two hours in average repair time." The team went for a quick hit and instituted that practice across the board.

But even if all the quadrants *averaged* a repair time of 19 to 20 hours, that still meant that too many potholes wouldn't be repaired within the one-day goal. So the team had to look for more solutions. They used what's called a cause-and-effects matrix (Figure 13) to help them identify other process factors that would have a big impact on repair time.

Figure 13:
Cause & Effects Matrix (excerpt)

Importance to customer		7	10	9	7	4	
Process Step	**Process Inputs**	Safer infrastructure	Cycle time	Increased cust. service	Repaired hole	Satisfied customer	Total
Complaint received	Trained dispatcher	3	9	9	3		249
	Complaint	3	0	1	1	0	37
	Citizen	0	3	1	1	0	46
Work order received	Web complaint	1	1	0	1	0	24
	Phone	1	1	0	1	0	24
	Correct info	9	9	3	1	9	223
Work order assigned to quadrant	Delivered work order	9	9	9	9	9	333
	Ass't Street Commissioner	9	3	3	9	3	195
	Weather (snow/rain)	3	3	3	9	3	153
	Available employee	3	9	0	3	3	144

To create a C&E matrix, the team identified important components of each step (listed down the side) and rated each as to how much it affected a desired outcome from that process (listed across the top). They then focused their attention on making sure that those high-impact components operated at peak performance.

Solutions & Results

The team decided to target the following areas for changes:

- Dispatcher operations and work assignments (how complaints were received, logged, and communicated to supervisors and crews). Changes made included:

    - Putting one person in charge of assigning all pothole complaints and checking for completion of work in all quadrants (this used to be done by all four supervisors)

    - Checking complaints more frequently—three times a day vs. once per day

    - Passing phoned-in complaints on to work crews immediately (though all trucks have communication equipment, it wasn't used to alert them about complaints prior to this project)

Bob Kennedy with street crew members Glen Williams (left) and Brett Hamilton (center).

- Increasing capacity. Changes made included:
  - Appointing a back-up person to monitor and assign complaints when other staff are out of the office.
  - Involving second and third shifts in pothole repair. Special lighting was added to the trucks so repairs could be made at night.
  - Expanding dispatcher and troubleshooter responsibilities to include repairing potholes on weekends and holidays when regular crews are not in.
  - Creating a special crew to do pothole repair work during the leaf collection season.

Results

Over the following two years:

- Repair times shortened quickly and dramatically, as shown in Figure 14 (improvement that has been sustained as shown in Figure 3 on p. 12)

Figure 14: Capability Improvements
Project inception through July 2005

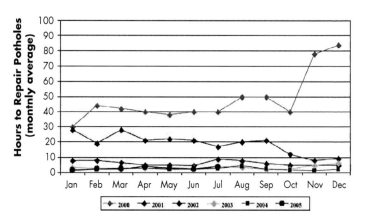

- Damage claims continued to drop (Figure 15)

Figure 15: Drops in Damage Claims

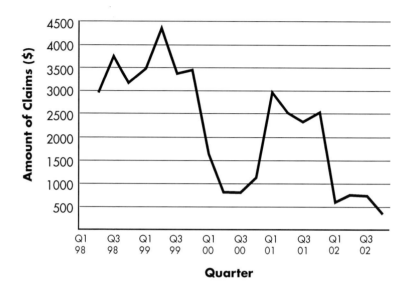

The amount of damage claims linked to potholes dropped dramatically as a result of this project.

What Made This Work

- **Waiting until the time was right.** We didn't tackle this project right out of the gate but rather timed it purposefully so that the head of the Street Department could build more rapport with staff—and actually get us to the point that when we did the project, we knew we could accomplish it. We have so many people looking over our shoulders that part of our challenge early on was making sure the projects we chose would help build trust and good spirit. Our first projects had to have significant impact and they had to be something we were confident we could successfully complete.

- **Data.** As noted, Bob comments that there were several ways in which what was actually happening differed from what everybody thought was going on. "Those were real eye-openers," he says.

- **People going the extra mile on their own.** "There were people from all over the country in my Black Belt class," recalls Bob. "They were all full-time Black Belts, so they had a lot more time to work on their projects. I'll never forget going into the second week of training, and they were *so* far ahead. Or, rather, I was so far behind. And I'm the kind of person who doesn't like to get behind. So several nights that week I sat up at a card table in my living room until 5 A.M., cranking through the project work."

Something new:
Performance-based incentives in government

For the first time ever, in 2001-2002, a performance-based incentive was added to the contract with the union workers in the Streets division. "This is a yearly bonus we pay out to workers based on about five performance target averages," explains Bob Kennedy. "The goals are set each year by a joint union-management committee. One key to our success has been setting high goals that are not easily attainable. Another is continually raising the performance standards."

The performance target for potholes has changed every year so far, he explains, and the payout amount has changed several times as well:

Contract Years	Repair target	Payout to worker
2001-2002	24 hrs	$200
2002-2003	12 hrs	$100
2003-2004	8 hrs	$100
2004-2005	3.5 hrs	$275
2005-2006	3.5 hrs	$175
2006-2007	3.5 hrs	$100
2007-2008	3.5 hrs	$100

"Setting that first target at 24 hours was a real battle," Bob recalls. "No one thought it was an achievable goal. We had the same battle over 12 hours the following year. But our performance has been so reliable that both union and management are confident we can meet a 3.5-hour target."

CHAPTER 2

The Paint
on the Canvas

Dr. Noriaki Kano, one of the key figures in the Japanese quality movement in the 1980s and 1990s, once commented to a group of American and Japanese consultants that American managers behave as if they are "starting with a blank canvas." In contrast, he continued, Japanese managers understand that every canvas has been painted many times already and the only realistic approach is to scrape away a few layers to expose what has gone before then to act accordingly.

As Mayor, my strategies for introducing Six Sigma had to rely on understanding the painted canvas that is the city of Fort Wayne. Here is a quick review that will help set the stage for the actions we took.

My Personal Landscape

I'm a life-long resident of Fort Wayne, a graduate of our North Side High School. I did leave the state briefly when getting my bachelor's from Princeton University. I served in the Indiana State Senate from 1974 until 1978, then spent most of the '80s and '90s in the private sector—though I stayed involved in state and local politics through advisory boards and community service agencies.

Perhaps most relevant to this book, there are two themes evident throughout my career:

1. I've always been interested in helping businesses grow and succeed:

   – I chaired the Indiana Institute for New Business Ventures, the Indiana Human Resources Investment Council and the Governor's Task Force on Small Business.

   – I was a partner in a firm that provided advisory services to business owners in management-led buyouts, capital sourcing and corporate turnarounds. I had my own consulting firm that helped business owners and executives develop their skills in business management, organizational development, and marketing.

   – I was a developer of the Fort Wayne Enterprise Center (Indiana's first industrial incubator).

2. I've always been a believer in bringing people together— to learn from each other, share resources, and work together to solve problems:

   – I helped develop the Northeast Indiana TQM Network, a not-for-profit learning cooperative with more than 40 member organizations, including large corporations, colleges, hospitals, and small businesses.

These factors, perhaps more than any other, have shaped what you'll see in this book. You'll see…

   • Just a sampling of many improvements we've made that contribute to more effective government—and a safer, healthier city in which to live and work.

   • New pathways for bringing people from various departments together, such as monthly meetings of department heads and training sessions with cross-department representation. Across the board, I hear that for many participants in these sessions, it's the first time they've met someone face-to-face whom they've been dealing with for years.

- A major emphasis on personal growth and learning (which, not coincidentally, feeds into our need for professional growth and learning). It's hard to put into words just how proud I am of all the people who stepped up to the plate, who, when given the opportunity, grabbed the initiative to learn and make their jobs and workplaces better.

The Historical Landscape: Rust Belt reborn

The second-largest city in Indiana, Fort Wayne is a city of more than 250,000 people in the northeast part of the state. As the name implies, it began life as a military fort back in the 1700s, named after General Anthony Wayne. The city was incorporated in 1840, and it was in the early 1900s that much of our infrastructure (water mains, roads) was laid down. (With this aging infrastructure, it should come as no surprise that one of our earliest Six Sigma projects was on water main replacement. See p. 213).

The city lies at the confluence of three rivers: the St. Joseph and St. Mary's rivers flow together to form the Maumee. Having a city founded on a strategic river system has been both a boon and a bane: easy river access contributed to the popularity of this location as a trading post, but the city is also prone to floods.

A city of rivers: the Columbia Street Bridge over the confluence of the St. Joseph and St. Mary's rivers, forming the Maumee River.

Major industries such as the Tokheim Pump Company, International Harvester, Inca Manufacturing (Phelps Dodge), Rea Magnet Wire, the Capehart Phonograph Company, and Magnavox opened in the 1920s. From there, the business history of Fort Wayne is revealed in a few simple facts: Thirty years ago, most graduates of local high schools planned on working at International Harvester (IH), General Electric, or other manufacturing plants after graduation, just as their fathers and grandfathers did. The IH plant closed in 1982, a victim of the rust-belt syndrome common in the upper Midwest. This is a legacy that cities like Fort Wayne have to work hard to overcome. We are working hard to replace the lost manufacturing jobs with advanced manufacturing, knowledge-based service businesses, and high-tech alternatives.

The Political Landscape

Indiana is largely what we now call a red state: traditionally Republican. The same is true of Fort Wayne. During the 2004 presidential election, for example, federally tracked political contributions to Republican causes outpaced those to Democrat causes by more than a 3-to-1 margin. My predecessor (a Republican) was elected to three consecutive terms. Recent opinion polls show Fort Wayne is the most conservative city in a very conservative state.

I am a Democrat.

As noted in Chapter 1, I won my first mayoral election in 1999 by 76 votes out of a total of 42,000 cast. Understandably, there was a recount and my opponent later sued over the results. But the totals stood, and I became the first Democratic mayor of Fort Wayne in 12 years.

People sometimes ask me about my political philosophy. I am a pro-business Democrat, but I also believe in the people in government. I believe in the importance of government to serve people.

You can't dislike government or the people in it and expect city employees to listen to you and hear your message.

You have to believe in the sincerity and talent of the people you have. As Mayor, it's my job to make sure they have the support they need to do the best job they possibly can.

The Organizational Landscape

Fort Wayne has more than 1,800 city employees. When I started my first term, I discovered the city government operated like most governmental units I've encountered. In business, I had become used to accomplishing goals through careful planning of work processes and practices. City government has traditionally been personality-based, not process-based, as this anecdote from one of our more recent hires illustrates:

"Until recently, Fort Wayne never had an emergency coordinator or planner. In the varied public safety departments, 'planning' was actually 'people.' Everyone just knew who did stuff in the departments and would call on particular people as needed. In 2002, when I was asked about the emergency plans for different events, the answer I got was 'Oh, we don't have one.' Well, I'd say, what do you do if an emergency happens? 'Well, Marty handles that.' And what if Marty isn't here? 'Well, Marty is always here.'"

Bernie Beier, Director of Homeland Security
for Fort Wayne

In short, a lot of work got done solely because we had a lot of very experienced, extraordinarily talented people on staff. But managers who operate with a Six Sigma mindset know that you can never achieve peak performance if you're relying on personalities or individuals. Work has to be studied, and the best practices documented and taught to everyone involved.

The Improvement Landscape (or, rather, the lack thereof)

"When Mayor Richard came into office. I had no idea what Six Sigma was. I thought it was a type of Karate—just kidding! ... But then I started looking at it and said, 'That would be interesting to do.' And I always like to do something different. It gives me a chance to learn something, and that's why I got involved in it. Then when it started saving money, I became even more interested."

Joe Johnson
Program Manager of Combined Sewer Overflow

Most private sector companies have evolved along with advances in the improvement methods; most public sector units have not.

General Electric (GE), for example, is one of the more prominent corporate users of Lean Six Sigma. Its interest in quality improvement dates back to the early 1980s when people started experimenting with "continuous improvement" and "total quality management." In the late '80s and early '90s, that evolved into Six Sigma, which imposed higher quality standards on performance and relied on new job positions (called "Belts") devoted exclusively to project work. By the mid-1990s, then-CEO Jack Welch realized that an element was still missing, and looked to adapt Lean practices (almost exclusively used in manufacturing at that time) to service and administrative processes. Lean methods are primarily focused on improving process speed by getting rid of waste. By the late 1990s, GE was using the full range of what we now consider to be Lean Six Sigma methods.

This evolutionary history means that people who have worked for GE for 5, 10, or 20 years have been exposed to quality thinking and tools in a number of guises. And even if they haven't worked directly on improvement teams, the language and principles of quality have permeated a lot of business practices. They're going to know what it means to "focus on the customer." They'll probably have seen process flowcharts posted in some work areas. In short, at least some elements of what they'll learn in Lean Six Sigma training will sound familiar to them. Many major corporations have a similar history with quality.

"We were so far behind in experience with quality that it was going to take a revolution, not an evolution, to bring us up to speed."

Roger Hirt
Master Black Belt and shaper of the
Six Sigma efforts in Fort Wayne

Roger Hirt (far right) reviews project reports with Jim Howard and Mary Saylor.

The opposite is true in most cities because few governmental units have done work with quality improvement.

Can you guess what the biggest problem is with this lack of experience with quality methods? By far the worst problem is that people inside city government have no reason to believe that *change*—and, more specifically, significant *improvement*—is really possible. They have never been allowed to challenge the status quo (at least not on the scale of rethinking work that's demanded by Lean Six Sigma). They haven't used or witnessed the application of Lean Six Sigma methods. They don't have peers inside other government agencies who can provide firsthand testimony.

All that had to change, and quickly, if we were to achieve the kind of results we needed. There's more on this topic in Chapter 5.

Conclusion

The rest of this book reflects decisions we made about when and how to weave Six Sigma into the everyday workings of city government in Fort Wayne. As you read through, keep in mind the various landscapes we were working with—my own history, the city's history, the political climate—and recognize that you'll likely make different decisions than my team and I did because your landscapes will be different. As Dr. Kano would say, you have to understand what's on your own painted canvas.

Featured Project #3

Slashing Red Tape

Despite the lack of experience with quality improvement (see previous chapter), the bright people who went through our Green Belt or Black Belt training picked up the essentials very quickly—and were often able to produce results through the use of a few simple tools. Here is a perfect example: a project led by Heather Presley, who works in the Economic Development department and is devoted to attracting more businesses and good jobs to the city.

"What I learned from this project is that most red tape revolves around communication breakdown," says project leader Heather Presley. "I've been with the city for 12 years, and what Six Sigma allowed us to do is stop the finger pointing and really understand what was going on with the process. Yes, we did some data collection, but the real gains came from simply getting people from a lot of different departments to talk about the process flow and make sure it all made sense."

Background

By 2001, Heather Presley had come to think of herself as "Complaint Central." Through her work in the Economic Development department, she'd been on the receiving end of stories about how difficult it was to do business with the city more times than she could count. That's why she jumped at the opportunity to serve on the new Red Tape Committee, charged with—what else—cutting red tape.

The Investigation

The committee began by interviewing local business owners, architects, and engineers, gathering what's called the Voice of the Customer (in Six Sigma terminology)—finding out what's important to them. One topic that rose to the top was the difficulty in getting site development permits approved. Large developers kept telling Heather that Fort Wayne's processes were too convoluted. "We're tired of having to bow at the counter," they'd say. Some were looking at other communities to do business with: "I'm not going to put myself through that hassle. The permit process takes too long, there are too many restrictions, and I'm not going to go in there and be treated that way."

Just how bad was the city's land improvement permit process? Initial benchmarking against other communities revealed that nearby smaller cities could turn around site plan improvement applications in just 5 to 10 days. Fort Wayne took nearly two months on average, with a large percentage dragging on for much longer (four to six months was not uncommon).

This is not the data you want to see or comments you want to hear if your job is to court business investments and attract new jobs. This is why Heather chose to attack this problem when she was asked by her boss to participate in the first Green Belt training offered by the city. Heather's boss, a veteran of contentious encounters with the many departments involved in permit approval, was frustrated and skeptical about the potential for success. She agreed to the project somewhat reluctantly and on the condition that Heather find someone else to be a champion for the project. So Andy Downs, chair of the Red Tape Committee and then-Chief of Staff to the Mayor, stepped in to fill that role.

"As it turned out," recalls Heather, "that was a critical development. I was a lowly Green Belt candidate, really just administrative staff at the time. I didn't have the power to make any changes. With 15 different departments involved—some city, some county—even my boss didn't have the authority it would take to make changes. So I really needed someone at Andy's level—and with his determination to 'make this happen'—in my corner."

Heather also admits that the project got off to a rocky start. "The zoning department, which really is the key point of contact for customers, initially refused to participate," she recalls. "They kept saying they didn't have time to be on a team." But, she continues, once they saw that the changes the team asked for would make *their* lives easier, they came on board and became full-fledged members of the team.

Team

Heather Presley, GB and project leader
Elissa McGauley, DED; Rick Kunkel, Planning
Michelle Kyrou, Development Services; Jim
Norris, Building Commissioner; Andy Downs,
Champion; Stacey Stumpf, BB

Defining the problem

A first step for this team was collecting the Voice of the Customer by conducting focus groups with representatives from other city departments affected by or involved in the permitting process, and with external customers (building contractors, engineers, and architects). What did these customers really want from the process?

- Timely approval of permits and certificates of compliance
- Excellent service in face-to-face contact
- Timely and accurate reviews
- Better communication between the city and the customer

To focus their efforts, the team created a process map (see Figure 14, next page) and answered the question, **"What process steps most significantly affect whether customers get what they want?"**

"We'd been doing customer interviews for years. But with the new administration, at last I had the chance to actually do something with that information, to make changes. It was really exciting!"

Heather Presley

They concluded that the following process elements were most critical:

- Reviews of the permit application documentation ("site packages")
- Routing meetings and attendees (where it is decided which city departments have to get involved in the review)
- Tools and guidelines used during reviews
- Communication back to the customer after the city's review

Figure 16: Permitting process Flowchart

Don't bother trying to read the fine print here. The visual impression is what's important. Originally, this process was very complicated, involving more than 20 steps and 15 man-hours of processing time.

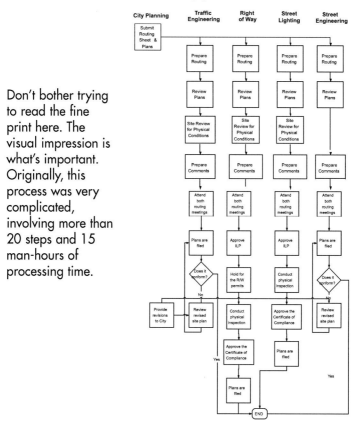

"The team wanted to know how many "touches" there were in the process—how many people were involved in reviewing the permits," says Heather. Their investigation revealed that there were a lot more touches than were needed. That meant the permit process was rife with wasted effort and delays. For example, standard practice had been to send every application to every department, when in reality different types of permits needed reviews by only certain departments. As the process was originally structured, a lot of people ended up reviewing a lot of permits they didn't have to.

Another problem was the number of times a permit had to loop through the process. For example, says Heather, after reviewing a permit, the zoning department would say, "We want landscaping on this property." Then stormwater would say, "Wait, you just changed the stormwater runoff. We've got to look at this again."

Solutions & Results

After studying each of the target process elements, the team came up with a number of process measurements, changes, and enhancements:

- Using a **punch list** to make sure that the permit requests are complete before they are accepted from the customer.
- Developing **better tracking** capability through the use of a new Access database (see Figure 17, next page) that Heather developed herself. Now anyone in the 15 departments can log into the system and check the status of a permit. That means a customer can get

an up-to-date answer no matter which department they contact. ("Because there was a mix of city and county departments who were going to use this database, we had to physically locate it on an offsite server," she recalls.)

- Developing **triaging criteria** (such as assigning "red flags" to permit types that had historically proved challenging or complex) and developing **alternative pathways** for simpler permit applications.

- Changing procedures to **provide better collaboration and communication** between city departments.

- **Collecting data regularly** to better measure and monitor turnaround times.

Figure 17:
Permit Tracker

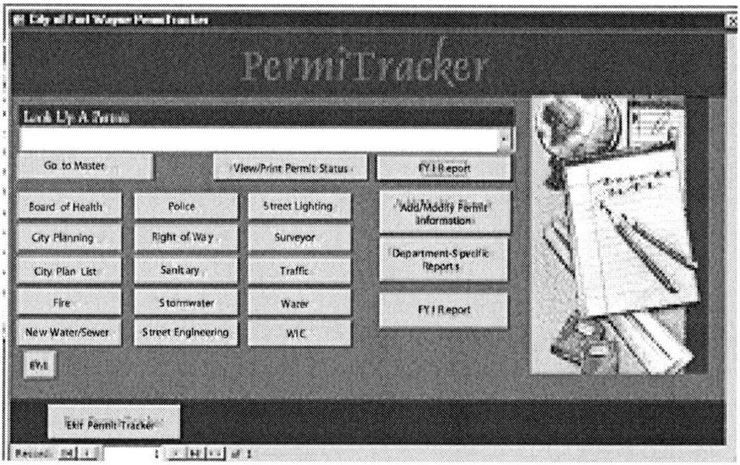

This is a screen capture of the new software program that Heather helped develop to make it easier to track where a permit was in the process. It is accessible by anyone involved in the process, making the city more responsive to a customer no matter whom he or she contacts.

"I can't overstate how important it was to have Andy's support throughout the project," says Heather. Her team would decide on process changes based on their analysis and inform all the departments. Some would make them, some wouldn't. "That's when Andy would step in," she adds, "and contact the departments himself. 'What part of these instructions didn't you understand?,' he'd ask. Then the changes would get made."

> "One of the innovative steps we started was to do a conceptual routing," says Heather. "A customer would say they've got an idea for something and different departments could look at it before they got very far into the project. The reviewers would often point out potential issues that the customer hadn't thought of, so they could make a better-informed decision about whether to go forward."

Results

The team tracked three different kinds of results: measurable improvements in lead time, cost avoidance, and anecdotal support.

1. Quantifiable results in lead time (Figure 18, Table A)

Figure 18:
Before/After Capability

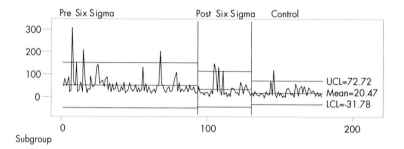

This type of graph is called a control chart. It shows each data point plotted in time order and three extra horizontal lines: the average or mean plus both an upper control limit (UCL) and lower control limit (LCL). The control limits indicate how much variation can be expected in the process. The narrow the limits, the better. Here, the control limits get closer together by the last phase of the project (that's good) and the average line has dropped as well (also good).

Table A	
Before	**After**
None released ≤14 days	95% released in ≤10 days
Nearly 1/4 took 60 days or more	Only "special causes" exceed 41 days
31 steps	7 steps (see Figure 19)
72 requests in the cycle	30 requests in the cycle

Figure 19: Site Plan Process After Improvements

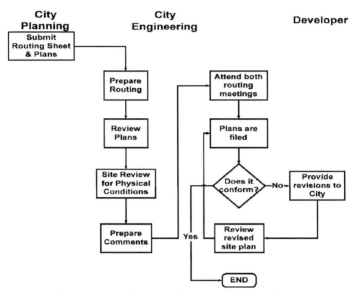

7 Steps, 2 1/4 man-hours per routing

The details here aren't important. Rather, compare the simplicity of this "after" process with the "before" process shown in Figure 14. There are only 7 steps compared to the original 31, which take just over 2 hours compared to more than 15 originally.

2. Expenditures avoided

By teaching herself Access and programming the new database, Heather saved the city $150,000 that was originally budgeted for software purchases (those funds were then put to other uses).

3. Anecdotal support

- Feedback from customers has entirely changed in tenor from "I said I'd never build here" to "I never believed that the city could get this good."

- The homebuilder's association was so excited about the gains that they invited Heather to give a presentation at an association meeting; she got rave reviews.

What Made This Work

- **Giving teams the green light to immediately fix obvious problems.** As Roger Hirt says, "One of our philosophies with all our Green Belts and Black Belts is that they shouldn't wait until the end of the project before making changes. Don't let it run on broken. We call it **process hardening**—get it done, put it in place, make it work, fix it."

- **Having a cross-functional team.** Typical permits need to pass through a number of city departments before they are approved, so no single department could have hoped to improve cycle time without cooperation from all the departments involved.

- **Using a process focus and data to build trust.** Team members drawn from different city departments were able to set aside historical finger-pointing blame games by focusing on the process and using data to isolate problems.

- **Making direct contact with customers.** Holding discussions with various customer groups (contractors, engineers, realtors) proved invaluable in providing direction and focus to the project, and in re-establishing trust between customers and the city.

Mini-Case: More red tape slashed

Maria Gomez-Espino, one of the many stars in our City Utilities department, has become one of our best Lean practitioners. While Six Sigma methods are mostly focused on quality, Lean methods work specifically on improving process speed and efficiency. Maria was able to eliminate some work steps entirely—a 100% reduction in time!—by analyzing the process flow and looking at which steps were needed and which weren't.

The project was based in the Contract Compliance department—the individuals who sign off during a construction project if the contractor has complied with the paperwork, such as weekly payrolls and wage scales. They need to make sure that the public paperwork is in before the Board of Works looks at the project to accept it. The contractors complained that getting a project signed off took too long and involved unnecessary approvals.

Maria began by mapping out the process from start to finish, identifying what steps the contract went through, what purpose those steps served, and how long it took. She discovered that in one process step an administrative assistant spent 90% of her time logging contractor payroll information into a spreadsheet that nobody used! She was flipping through hundreds of pages of daily payroll documents when there was no need to do so. Guess what? That work was non-value-added and unnecessary—so it was eliminated. Does that mean the department had to let the assistant go? No chance. There was plenty of other valuable work for her to do in the department. She was trained for new duties within the department, which turned out to be a great learning experience.

Overcoming the fear of punishment

In companies that have never adopted improvement methods, people are going to be suspicious when someone (especially a department outsider) comes in and starts asking about their work, asking how things operate, timing the steps, questioning why things are done a certain way, and seeking changes. In our case, that kind of investigation had rarely happened; in the private sector, outside the context of improvement, it has often been the prelude to reorganization and layoffs.

The only way to get beyond these natural reactions is to keep emphasizing that the purpose is to improve, not punish. You have to follow that up with actions consistent with that promise.

As Maria says, "I was an outsider coming into an area to understand its functions and help improve the process. So I jumped right in. Of course, a lot of people felt intimidated at first, wondering what I was 'really' trying to do. They tend to think the negative, 'Are you going to get rid of me?'"

But, she continues, "I continued to explain the goal and why I was there. We got through it. I asked them to be open and honest, and to share with me how the process happens, so I can understand it better. Then, we can identify improvements and work together as a team to improve them. And it worked."

CHAPTER 3

"Who Is Your Customer?"

and other secrets of thinking like a business owner

When Roger Hirt (a Master Black Belt from GE) or Michele Hill (our first Black Belt) or I would talk with department managers about how we wanted to start using Six Sigma and Lean methods, some people were excited about the opportunities. But more common reactions were statements like:

- "We don't make a product, so why do we have to worry about reducing costs? What difference does it make what something costs?"
- "You keep talking about customers, but I don't have any customers."
- "We're not a factory. We don't make things."
- "We provide services. This stuff doesn't apply to us."

Many people could not see how Lean and Six Sigma could be used to improve their jobs. That failure is symptomatic of a fundamental problem in the public sector: there is little appreciation of how individual jobs link together or just how much more efficient and effective we can be.

The Big Shifts

From inward to outward,
from status quo to constant improvement

Marcel Proust once said, "The real voyage of discovery consists not in seeking new landscapes but in having new eyes." Our challenge was to get city government leaders and employees seeing our business in a very different way, looking outward.

Not coincidentally, the two most important business practices I wanted to bring to city government also happened to be core themes of Six Sigma.

1. Like the majority of businesses just a few decades ago, government operations tend to be very inward focused. Employee jobs and goals are defined based almost solely on what the department manager thinks is important. People know that their work goes "somewhere" when they are done, but they don't know what matters in that "somewhere" place. In contrast, Six Sigma practitioners know that only customers—the people in the "somewhere" black hole—can define what quality is and therefore what matters most about the work we do.

2. Perhaps because we often work in the public eye and much of our work is governed by laws, city government is a very conservative enterprise. The goal is to maintain the status quo because that's the safest path. By definition, improvement involves change. So you'll never get Six Sigma embedded in your city until people start to embrace change and the potential for doing things differently.

Talk to anyone whose name appears in this book—not to mention the dozens of other people involved in changing our city government whose stories we didn't have space to include—and they'll tell you that establishing a new vision doesn't happen easily or quickly. As the leader of this organization called city government, my role is to help drive that change process by making clear what I expect of the people who report to me and of all city employees.

To help people see challenges in a new way, I often ask key questions when I meet with city employees. Some of my favorites are:

1. **Who is your customer? Who benefits from or uses your work?** The people who can easily answer this question are those who have direct contact with residents and business owners. But many city employees never have direct contact with anyone outside government. Does that mean they don't have customers? Far from it! Every single one of us has customers—either we hand off our work directly to someone else or the outcome of our work affects someone, somewhere. Knowing who these customers are and what they care about should be the starting point for all business decisions.

2. **Are you constantly getting better? How do you know?** In business there is very little room for maintaining the status quo (see sidebar). If you aren't changing—constantly getting better at providing what customers want and improving cycle times and quality—you'll be left behind by your competitors. With increasing demand by citizens to do more and increasing pressure to hold down taxes and fees, city governments need to adopt that same mindset. If you ask most people today if they are getting better, doing better work, most will answer yes. Trouble

is, they have no data or evidence to back up that claim. That's why the follow-up question—how do you know?—is perhaps more important than the first. Each time I give my annual Report to the People, the presentation is filled with data that not only shows where we are today but also how much we've improved over time. (See the data charts at the end of Chapter 1, pp. 12-15, for example.) I demand the same evidence-based thinking among city employees.

Other New Factors in the Equation

Nailing down the first two new ways of seeing problems—starting to be concerned with customers and using data as proof of improvement—is a great start to achieving operational excellence. But other changes in thinking must occur to get you all the way there. Three that you'll see evident in the case studies featured in this book are:

A. Adopting a systems view

B. Thinking about costs

C. Becoming a learning organization

A. Adopting a Systems View

What happens in each department affects the whole organization

Every traditional company complains about the pervasive "silo" mentality that prevents people in different departments from talking to each other or collaborating to share knowledge and information. I found the silo mentality to be even stronger in city government than in most businesses: people were very much focused solely on their jobs or their departments and there was very little concern for or communication with people in other departments.

This separation of one job from another, of one department from another, is incompatible with quality-driven performance. To provide excellent customer service while still cutting costs and time, the various parts of your organization have to talk with each other. The reasons why are explained by the (relatively) new vision of organizations as dynamic systems where what happens in each part affects the whole. Understanding systems thinking is key to shaping high-performance government, and I'd highly recommend the works of Peter Drucker and Peter Senge.

> *"We are trying to develop a culture where there are habitual expectations for continuous improvement. People can take risks in the organization, and failures from taking those risks are not seen as opportunities for punishment, but really opportunities to learn. It helps problem solving. The organization has a systems approach to everything—we are not just looking at little bits and pieces, but at the whole organization as a system, a lot like the human body is a system."*
>
> Kate Love-Jacobson
> Professional Development & Quality Enhancement
> Manager

B. Thinking About Costs

A few weeks into my first year as Mayor, I kept seeing a lot of cars with the insignias of different city departments just parked in the city lots. I asked department heads why those cars just sat there—if the cars weren't being used, why was the city carrying that excess inventory? The answer was that some departments weren't using the cars designated for their department heads or other staff.

> *"Why don't people in other departments use them then?" I asked.*
>
> *"Because they have the wrong insignia," came the reply.*
>
> *"Do you mean that each department is so focused on its own image that it won't use a car with a wrong insignia?"*
>
> *"Right."*
>
> *"So," I continued, "if all the vehicles had a generic city insignia, then they'd get used more?"*
>
> *"Yes."*

This discussion led to a re-evaluation of the city's policy on take-home cars across all departments (except those involved in public safety). The result: we were able to slash the number of take-home cars from 60 to just 6. The other 54 cars were either added to the general city fleet or sold off. That move freed up $317,000 in the budget.

Examples like this demonstrated the need for people in city government to become more cost conscious. Historically, city employees rarely thought about issues like activity-based costing, which has become common practice in private sector businesses. But now, for example, we're talking about how much it costs to maintain the parks system on a dollar-per-acre basis. That transition to activity-based costing and management is still a work in progress. We are training employees to think in terms of how much it costs to do our work rather than how much of the budget we have to spend.

Building that kind of basic business mentality—getting the most out of the dollars we're spending—proved to be almost as fruitful as any specific Lean Six Sigma efforts.

The Ultimate Twist:
Selling city services to private enterprises

The continuing annexation of nearby communities means that our city departments now have to serve almost 40% more residents. To do that without adding staff means there is a lot of pressure on city departments to get more efficient at their core tasks. Fort Wayne recently switched 80,000 customers to a new "drive-by" wireless digital water meter reading system. Pat Faherty in our Meter Reading department built on the gains from that switch by leading a project to raise the average number of meter reads from about 680 per hour to over 800 per hour. As a result of the increased efficiency, the remaining meter reading staff was reduced from 10 people to 2 (the 8 people were moved into other city departments). Most astonishingly, we are now so good at meter reading that we are marketing that service to private utilities.

C. Becoming a Learning Organization

The most dynamic companies have learned how to become **learning organizations.** These are enterprises where, as Peter Senge puts it, people continually expand their capacity to create the results they truly desire, where new and expansive patterns of thinking are nurtured, where collective aspiration is set free, and where people are continually learning to see the whole together. In a learning organization, taking the time to educate yourself is not just *accepted*, it is *expected* in every job. The learning can come in many forms: looking at data from inside your organization to get a better understanding of its functioning, attending a training session, reading books, talking to industry experts, interacting with co-workers about improvement, or visiting companies that are doing good work in some area relevant to your business.

Having a mental attitude of excellence in learning keeps the best business leaders on the forefront of their industries. It makes them willing to explore new ideas. Paul Spoelhof, who works in our community development department, has experienced firsthand the conversion of Fort Wayne government to a learning organization. He describes it this way:

> *"I've been in other jobs where the expectation was that you came into the position knowing everything you needed to know. That was the pervasive attitude. So people didn't talk about what they didn't know. Any new ideas that came from new guys like me were thought of as 'cute' and we were 'young and naïve' ... I was blown away by the concept of learning organi-*

zations and the idea that the next better idea or process or improvement won't be discovered unless someone is pushing the envelope of what they know and understand.... I'm in a position now where I can encourage people to understand new things."

This new attitude has profoundly affected the work of Paul's department, and others as well. Here's Paul again with an example of this impact:

"When I first started, there was very little coordinated, comprehensive understanding of the city's approach to housing. None of the things we were doing were bad, but everything was happening in a vacuum," he says. But once the department took on a learning mentality, things began to change. "We got involved so we could understand what housing means in Fort Wayne and how it's related to a healthy community. Now, fully half of our department is devoted to housing and housing services—it's the complete housing picture, not just housing for the poorest people."

In business, the phrase "thinking out of the box" is probably overused. But I think the concept of building a learning organization has helped city employees do a lot of out-of-the-box thinking by allowing them to move beyond the limitations of how work has always been done. Jim Howard, the city's Director of Purchasing and an attorney, has done a lot of box-breaking on his own. "One of the things we did was work with departments to brainstorm ways to get more group rates on our purchases. And we came up with the idea of creating a p-card system, which works just like a credit card, for small purchases. We give the p-cards to people who make small purchases, and everything gets tracked.

Not only does that information enable us to bundle small purchases, but we also qualified for rebates in 2005 with $1 million of small purchases."

In addition to the effective use of the p-card, Jim has found savings through consortium spending, where groups (such as the Fort Wayne Community Schools and Allen County) pool their resources to get more buying power. Jim explains there are areas of common interest, such as uniforms, copiers, road salt, natural gas, and diesel fuel, where joint buying leads to significant savings.

Once this notion took hold, the purchasing department looked for other opportunities for bundling individual purchases and for joining with other governmental entities. "One of our biggest expense areas was vehicles," says Jim. "We did some exploring and contacted General Motors, who told us that it was much easier for them to bid on large national contracts than on state and local contracts. So we came up with the idea of creating a master bid for all the

Chet Shastri, Superintendent of the Water Filtration Plant and one of our Green Belts, says, "The learning environment at the city has improved quite a bit. I'm encouraging all my employees to go through whatever training they can.... Aside from Six Sigma, we are trying to make other changes at the water treatment plant. That's where I think learning becomes important."

vehicles we would buy for an entire year. We used federal specifications for those vehicles. That had never been done by a local government before. The vehicle list was comprehensive and included Allen County's needs as well. The final contract was made available to any other governmental entity within the State of Indiana. The pricing we ultimately got was far superior to even the state bids, and now other municipalities are contacting us to see if they can buy through our contract."

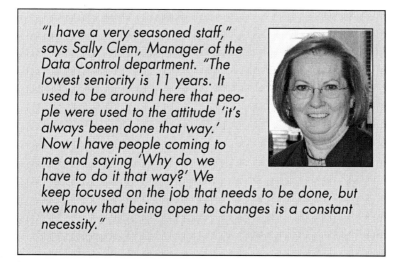

"I have a very seasoned staff," says Sally Clem, Manager of the Data Control department. "The lowest seniority is 11 years. It used to be around here that people were used to the attitude 'it's always been done that way.' Now I have people coming to me and saying 'Why do we have to do it that way?' We keep focused on the job that needs to be done, but we know that being open to changes is a constant necessity."

You'll read about some of our formal education programs in later chapters, but equally important is the way that people have run with the idea of continuous learning. For example, after completing our leadership development program (see Ch. 4), Mary Jane Slaton and Maria Gomez-Espino decided to start a book discussion group of their own. "We wanted to read one book every quarter and get together for lunch every other week to talk about how what we were reading related to what we are doing in our jobs," says Mary Jane. "We haven't done as much as we'd like but so far we've read Jim Collins's *Good to Great*, books on leading employees, and some of the *One Minute Manager* books." In addition, Mary Jane says she checks the Internet several times a week looking for articles related to something she's working on at the moment.

One More Shift: From limitations to possibilities

The content of this book describes a number of fundamental changes in how government operates in the city of Fort Wayne. One of the most gratifying is the new energy I see around what's possible.

Kate Love-Jacobson puts it this way: "We've always been told why we can't do things, what the constraints are, what the financial problems are. And I think the biggest boon derived from all this is that people are feeling empowered to imagine and dream. We think about the possibilities of what we can be and what we can offer to citizens—instead of feeling constrained by legislation, finances, or bureaucracy." She's not alone in her opinion:

"The mayor's vision is very infectious. He has a lot of insight into what our community COULD be, and he's empowering us to make things better. It's an exciting time to work for government."

Gina Kostoff, Utility Services Manager

"For a long time, we were just busy 'getting work done' every day and managing projects... what's been fun and enlightening over the past couple of years is that we have the time, resources, and permission to also look at HOW we get things done."

Mary Jane Slaton, Project Manager for Stakeholder Relationships

Lessons Learned #2

1. **We should have worked sooner on the broader business skills/awareness** — As discussed in this chapter, our challenge wasn't just learning about Lean and Six Sigma, it was establishing some basic business functions. Over time, it became increasingly clear that the lack of good business practices and a lack of individual leadership skills hampered our ability to push Lean Six Sigma. We now see how much it would have helped if we had done more to build these foundation practices and leadership skills earlier in the deployment.

2. **We should have started sooner on building a culture of learning** — Looking back, I think our Lean and Six Sigma efforts would have moved faster had I established new norms around learning at the executive levels. For example, our well-received four-day Mayor's Leadership Development Roundtable (see Ch. 4) was initiated in January 2004. Earlier availability of this kind of dynamic and energizing learning experience would have helped build acceptance of Six Sigma and promote systems thinking.

Conclusion

Pick up any book on Six Sigma and the description will likely include words like "cut waste" and "improve customer satisfaction." In Fort Wayne and, I suspect, most other cities, those words don't seem relevant to city employees. Creating an environment where people *want* to know how to evaluate their work against customer needs and *want* to know they're getting better and better is a prerequisite for creating a pull for Six Sigma. (More on this issue in chapters 6 and 7.)

Featured Project #4

The Science of Sludge

Our waste water treatment facility is the closest we come to operating a manufacturing plant. Like many of our private sector counterparts, we were up against an entrenched mentality that "this has been working for 40 years, we don't need to fix anything." That didn't daunt project leader Cheryl Cronin, who completed this project as part of her Black Belt certification. As you'll see, a combination of getting people in the same room together to talk about what they do (one of my favorite themes in this book) and detailed data analysis helped us to exceed the original goal by 300%.

You'll see reference in this project to "Class A sludge." These are biosolids that have been "digested" (held and heat-treated) for 15 days so that they meet specific contaminant and other criteria set by the EPA. As such, they can be processed and used for various purposes. We routinely give away and/or sell 30,000 tons of biosolids (sludge) per year. The material is used for gardens and soil amendments for lawns.

By keeping the sludge Class A, this project allowed us to complete the environmental loop and have our final waste water plant residuals used in an environmentally friendly way. Without Class A sludge we would still be incurring very high costs to have the material incinerated or hauled away to a hazardous-waste landfill. The project also allowed us to defer $1.7 million in repair expenditures. The group also saved so much time that they can now get a lot more work done. And a lot of people were given the chance to grow professionally. We couldn't ask for anything more.

"When I first started at this facility," says Cheryl Cronin, "only the superintendent had control over what was going on. He had all this data coming to his office every day. Nobody at the plant knew what it meant, only him. And he was in control of everything.

"It's not like that anymore. I want the people working with the process every day to feel ownership. And that's one thing that this project and all our other projects helped us accomplish. Now instead of people of coming in and saying, 'I have this problem, solve this for me and call me when you've got the solution,' they come into my office with process maps and say, 'Can we try this?' Or they say, 'I've been seeing something I think is a problem, but I think we can do X, Y, Z and it will get better. Can I have your permission to try this?' It's still a struggle in some sense to get more shared accountability, but this culture shift has been huge—and we did it in just a few short years."

Cheryl Cronin with one of the "digesters" used in the production of sludge.

Background

The waste water treatment plant in Fort Wayne opened in 1940. And, says project leader Cheryl Cronin, it pretty much operated the same way for the next 55 years. The goal is to turn waste water into clean water by removing volatile compounds and other contaminants, and then discharge it back into a stream. This happens in six steps.

1. Waste water enters the plant and large debris is screened out.

2. Grit is removed.

3. The waste water then goes into the **primary clarifiers** where most of the solids are settled out and become **sludge.**

4. The waste water is piped into huge aeration tanks where **bacteria** are cultured. The bacteria clump together to form a biomass (called **activated sludge**).

   – At the Fort Wayne plant, the bacteria are most efficient when they are about 10 days old—that means staff have to keep removing a portion of the activated sludge in a process called "wasting" to make room for new, younger bacteria. (The portion removed is called **waste activated sludge** or **W.A.S.** It is this W.A.S. that was the subject of this project.)

5. Ideally, the W.A.S. is **thickened** by being pumped into a huge **centrifuge** that separates the sludge (including the aging bacteria) from clear water.

6. The W.A.S. solids are then piped into a digester where they decompose. If they meet certain EPA standards after "digestion," they are Class A sludge and can be used as a soil amendment product or agricultural fertilizer.

The Investigation

At the start of this project, one of the key problems was that the centrifuges were run only about 50% of the time, which meant the W.A.S. being fed into the digesters contained a lot of water. This excess water consumed a lot of space in the digester, which, in turn, limited how much Class A sludge the plant could produce.

Therefore, the original goals for the project were to:

- Increase the centrifuge usage from 50% to 90% (meaning 90% of the W.A.S would be processed instead of just 50%).
- Increase total solids (TS) in the W.A.S. from 2.2% to 4.0%. TS is a measure of how thick the sludge is. The thicker the better—at least up to a certain limit; thicker means that more water has been reclaimed.

As you'll see, both of these goals were changed later in the project, but for very different reasons.

Team
Ted Rhinehart, Champion; Ned Byrer, Financial; Cheryl Cronin, Black Belt; Brian Panzer, Mechanic; Gwen Bard, Process Analyst; John Kohne, Laboratory; Mike Glymph, Operator; Jeff Vachon, Operator; Chris Gach, Technical

Phase 1: Define the process

In the Six Sigma improvement methodology, one of the first steps is to document how the process currently works. This step proved to be eye-opening for the entire team. Here's one clue about why: there were eight operators working the centrifuge. Care to guess how many different ways there were of running the equipment? You got it— eight!

They discovered this fact after Cheryl had each operator write down how they did their job. Then they all looked at the results. "I think even the operators were surprised at just how differently they were each running the equipment," says Cheryl. "I think they thought they all had the same basic idea about how it should be done, and it wasn't that way at all."

To start working through this confusing situation, the team divided the work into individual steps. Then together all eight operators started looking at all the ways in which step 1 was done. "And I told them, we could only pick one of these ways because we want everybody to do it the same," Cheryl says. "It may not be THE right way, but we want everybody to do it ONE way because that's the only way to take out all this other variation."

Not surprisingly, the final map was a combination of best practices from all eight operators. "We found out that one guy did one thing well and another guy did another thing well," recalls Cheryl. "So we mixed and matched until we found something that made sense and was something that everybody could do."

Can you guess what happened next?

"As soon as we got everybody doing things the same way, the total solids measured in the W.A.S. coming out of the centrifuge jumped from 2.2% to 5.0%," says Cheryl. "That was above our original goal of 4.0%." (See Figure 20, next page.)

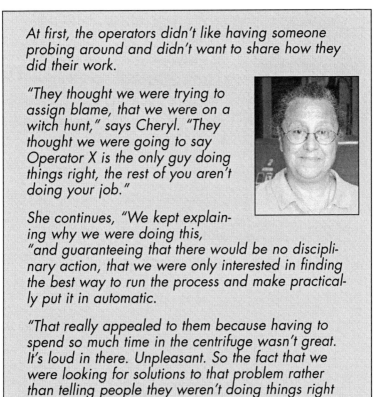

At first, the operators didn't like having someone probing around and didn't want to share how they did their work.

"They thought we were trying to assign blame, that we were on a witch hunt," says Cheryl. "They thought we were going to say Operator X is the only guy doing things right, the rest of you aren't doing your job."

She continues, "We kept explaining why we were doing this, "and guaranteeing that there would be no disciplinary action, that we were only interested in finding the best way to run the process and make practically put it in automatic.

"That really appealed to them because having to spend so much time in the centrifuge wasn't great. It's loud in there. Unpleasant. So the fact that we were looking for solutions to that problem rather than telling people they weren't doing things right was a key part of our message."

Figure 20:
Initial Gains in Percent Solids

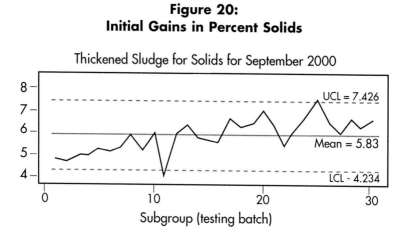

Thickened Sludge for Solids for September 2000

This chart shows measurements of sludge thickness over the course of the initial part of the project. As you can see, the line has an upward trend, which is good because higher numbers means thicker sludge (which was one project goal).

Phase 2:
Setting the sights higher

Since the team had already exceeded their goal, they could have stopped there.

"But that got us thinking," continues Cheryl. "Maybe there were more ways to go. So we looked at what the maximum thickness was that the sludge pumps could handle, and reset our goal at 6% to 8% total solids."

With this new goal in sight, the team continued working through the Six Sigma method, using data to explore theories about how to best control the process within the targeted range.

At this point the team discovered that they were very good at making either really thin sludge or really thick sludge— as shown by the two clusters of tall bars in Figure 21 (next page). Unfortunately, they wanted the sludge thickness to fall in the middle (between the tall bars and near the peak of the curve).

Figure 21:
Data on Percent Solids

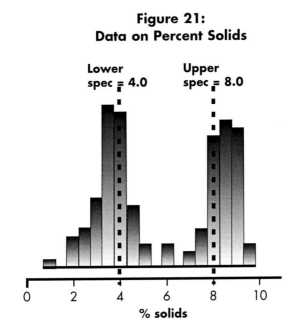

The pattern in this bar chart shows that originally the water treatment plan was very good at producing either very thin sludge (the peak to the left) or very thick sludge (the peak to the right). The ideal, however, would be to have a single peak right in the middle.

Solutions & Results

To solve the problem of too-thin or too-thick sludge, the team came up with a list of the factors they thought would give them the most control over total solids, and performed a series of sophisticated statistical analyses to determine which factors were most important. "Originally we gathered data about how the process was run," explains Cheryl. "At this point, we started doing experiments to manipulate certain factors—that way we could actually quantify the effect of things like how fast we pumped sludge into the centrifuge and how fast the centrifuge would spin." A chart of the main results is shown in Figure 22.

Figure 22:
Experiment Results

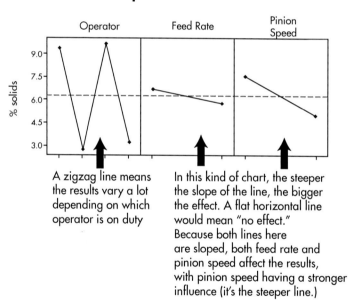

They discovered that:

- Pinion speed (the rate at which the centrifuge spins) is a "coarse knob"—it will help them get in the right ballpark

- Feed rate into the centrifuge is a "fine knob"—changing the feed rate at a given pinion speed will help them reach a target thickness for the sludge
- Unfortunately, there were still big differences between operators, and those differences had a big effect on the outcome

Dealing with operator variation

The particular kind of statistical analysis used in this project helps people sort out the sources of variation. It helps you see not just how much things are changing all the time but also what accounts for those changes. One key chart from this analysis is shown in Figure 23, which depicts the variation patterns for four different operators. The following text explains each pattern.

Figure 23:
Data Reflects Actual Practice

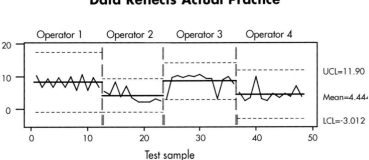

These data points show two days of continuous operation of the centrifuge, with four operators each working a 12-hour shift.

- The first shift shows data points alternating up and down. While some up-and-down is expected, this sawtooth pattern (a shift in direction at each data point) never occurs naturally (unless you're mixing data from two different sources). In this case, the operator checked the centrifuge once an hour throughout his shift and tweaked the settings every single time.

- When the second operator took over, he made adjustments for the first few hours (shown again by the up-and-down pattern), then let the process go without adjustments. By leaving the equipment alone, the operator was allowing the sludge to get thinner and thinner (seen as the line drifting downward)—this made it easier for him to pump out the sludge at the end of his shift.

- When the third operator came on, he saw that the sludge was thin and adjusted the centrifuge so the sludge would thicken. He then let the process run under these new settings without further adjustment for a number of hours (notice how little variation there is). Then a few hours before the end of his shift,

---

"One really critical thing we stumbled on at this stage was finding out that the meter reading labeled as Load on the centrifuge was really a reading of total solids," says Cheryl. "Until then, nobody knew what Load was."

What's so important about discovering the meaning behind a gauge? "Before then, the only way we could measure total solids in the tank was to take a sample and get it measured in the lab. The results would come back a day later—which meant our operators were making adjustments based on what happened yesterday! Being able to get an immediate reading on the effect of changes in our process was tremendously helpful."

he ran the sludge light for an hour (again, to make it easy to pump). But he didn't want to leave it that way so he made a few more adjustments near the end so the sludge thickness was nearer the target for the start of the next shift.

- The fourth operator was essentially doing the same thing as the first operator—making a lot of adjustments—only not as often. There is still a sawtooth pattern, but it isn't as pronounced.

What was critical about this chart is that Cheryl could tell what the operators were doing during their shift just by looking at the data patterns. Every manipulation showed up. And it's not that these guys were doing anything wrong; this was how they had been taught to run the process.

"This chart was actually a huge win for us," says Cheryl, "because we finally convinced the operators that we could see what they were doing—and that what they were doing made a difference. It also showed that the new procedures let us look at real-time information and determine *right now* if they were making thick sludge or thin sludge. This convinced them that they really, really, really all needed to be doing the same thing!"

> *We went from using "I think so" or "I've been here 40 years, are you questioning me?" to "the data says this is what we do." We make decisions about process changes according to data.*
>
> *Cheryl Cronin, Black Belt*

Results

The overall results from this project are shown in Table B.

Table B: Sludge Project Results		
	1999	2000
Average Thickened Sludge =	2.2%	8.2%
% of Time Sludge is Centrifuged =	44.9%	82.2%
Detention Time =	7.3 days	15 days
Volatile Solids Reduction =	44%	67.9%
Fuel costs =	$8,200	$244

As you can see, Cheryl's team managed to:

- Get the sludge almost four times thicker than it was originally (and twice the original goal).

- Run the centrifuge more than 80% of the time, compared to just 45% originally. This was important because thicker sludge makes the process much more efficient.

- Double the detention time for the sludge from 7 days to 15 days. Because the sludge was thicker, the digester tanks didn't fill up so quickly, and the processed sludge could be held more than twice as long. This is important because the EPA requires that sludge be detained a minimum of 15 days in order to be classified as Class A Sludge.

- Remove even more "volatile solids." This is another factor related to the production of Class A Sludge and environmental health. The minimum amount of reduction required by EPA is 38%; as you can see, the process was barely above this originally but well above that mark by the end.

- Save almost $8,000 in fuel costs (which will be annu-
al savings!). This was an unanticipated benefit from
the project. Methane is a natural byproduct of the
bacterial digestion process. Once the process
increased in efficiency, the system produced enough
methane to almost fully fuel itself.

What happened to the goal
of 90% centrifuge operations?

You may recall that another goal for the project originally
was to get to a point where the centrifuge was operating
90% of the time. At the end of the project, they achieved
only 82.2%. Was that a failure?

"Once we got into the project, we realized that the original goal of 90% wasn't realistic," explains Cheryl. "We
had failed to account for natural events like floods or big
rain events. During those time, we can't run the centrifuge. So achieving 82% operation is just about as good
as we can get."

What Made This Work

- **Patience:** This sludge operation had been run basically
the same way for decades. Never before had anyone been
asked to analyze what was happening and why, or make
systematic changes for the purposes of improvement and
control. So it's quite understandable that the staff were
not only resistant to but also suspicious of change. It
took patience and delivery of a consistent message to

convince the operators that the purpose was improvement, not blame or punishment.

- **Involving the people who worked the equipment.** Just imagine what would have happened if Cheryl had come in one day and told the operators that she had a new and better way of running this operation and that they were all to do things *her* way. Letting the operators talk with each other about what they did and why, and collectively decide on *one* new method, served several goals: it respected the expertise they'd gained from years on the job, it gave them ownership of the changes, and it made it more likely that the changes would be implemented.

- **Data and experiments.** Once the initial process standards were set, all subsequent changes were based on what the data showed. Since the goal was to find the best way to run the process, the team had to conduct experiments—not just rely on data gathered as the process normally operated. The experiments allowed them to determine which control factors had the biggest impact on sludge thickness and how those factors should be set to keep the sludge thickness within the target range.

What to do with the extra time

Before this project, every operator spent four to five hours per shift in the centrifuge control room. Now, it's an hour. That doesn't mean they have time to twiddle their thumbs or that the plant can lay off a worker.

"Having to spend only an hour per shift dealing with the centrifuge is a good thing," says Cheryl. "We have PLENTY of work that just wasn't getting done before. Now we can spend time on education; the operators have time to do preventative maintenance. They can pay attention to lab results. We've changed the scope of their job. This didn't mean we needed fewer people—it meant we can use our resources better and get *more* work done *better.*"

CHAPTER 4

The Leadership Iceberg

There's a lot more potential than you think

"The leadership development course helped me appreciate the difference between leading and managing. There are a lot of managers who aren't good leaders and a lot of good leaders who don't have the title of manager. Leaders are distinguished by their ability to get things done and get people excited."

Mary Jane Slaton

"During the leadership training, what stuck out for me was what Stephen Covey calls Principle-Centered Leadership. It's important to have values and model them, not just talk about them. I learned about the importance of relationships and communication, and the need to appreciate the roles of different departments and people.

Matthew Wirtz

I've always believed that if you give people opportunity for leadership, they will run with it; that the leadership you see in most organizations is just the tip of the iceberg; that there is a vast pool of untapped talent in every organization that will shine through if people are given training, technology, and the tools to do their jobs smarter and better.

Mary Jane and Matthew are just two of many examples we have in Fort Wayne to support that belief. There are dozens of city employees who have taken the initiative to get educated in Six Sigma, to solve problems plaguing their departments, to keep learning and improving. You only need read the many cases studies in this book to get an idea of what these people can accomplish when given the chance.

I am NOT in the business of creating leaders. People have to decide within themselves that they are willing to take risks, to push further, to learn more. As I've said before, my job is to create opportunities for people to assume the role that I call a "learning leader," someone who is tirelessly vigilant in the pursuit of excellence in all its meanings.

Specific Support Mechanisms

In this chapter I want to focus on two key support mechanisms:

1. Our Leadership Development Roundtable, where everyone from department heads to frontline staff can learn the keys to becoming a positive force in the workplace
2. Helping managers and supervisors become better sponsors and champions for our improvement efforts

1. Mayor's Leadership Development Roundtable

"I was in the first wave of people who went to the leadership round-table. When I first got picked I thought, 'Another training. What are we doing?' But I really liked it. You learn about yourself. I learned how to be a better manager and a leader, and how those are two different things. You also have contacts with different departments.... It was a really good experience."

Valerie Ahr

"I had the privilege of participating in the first wave of the leadership roundtable. I was very happy [with the roundtable] because the city never had this kind of focused training opportunity in the past. Usually, development training is within your own division related to your job, so you don't really interact with someone from a different area. The roundtable allows for individual learning and development, but also brings a lot of different people together.... We brainstorm together and develop things together. That's the best part. You meet people from different departments, you get a concept of what they do and how you may relate to that. And we knew the initiative was coming directly from the Mayor."

Maria Gomez-Espino

I'm letting Valerie and Maria speak for me because they said exactly what I would have said to describe the purpose of the Mayor's Leadership Development Roundtable (MLDR). As you can probably tell, the core issue is about a lot more than just learning some improvement tools and methods. What's needed for a city or any enterprise to succeed is a "learning culture"—people who are constantly seeking out new knowledge, who are able to learn and adapt. This might also be called an "innovation" or "creative" culture. For a long time now, government employees have had limited opportunities to take initiative, to be innovative about how their work gets done. But that is exactly what's needed to make cities competitive.

I think we all know that change of this magnitude won't happen by having me stand on a soapbox. It will happen only when others...

- Appreciate the need for change
- Have an understanding of what needs to change
- Are solicited for input on how to create the change
- Are given the knowledge and skills to be better tomorrow at what they're doing today

And that is the purpose of the MLDR. It's a vehicle for getting people excited about their own potential, for giving them some fundamental tools to become leaders, no matter where they are in the organization, manager or not. It is another mechanism for inspiring and engaging the hearts and minds of ordinary people.

There's another purpose as well. One of the MLDR participants, a long-time city employee, stopped me in the hall one day and said, "I've just finished reading Peter Senge's *Fifth Discipline*, and now I finally got the theory behind what you're trying to do." He had always been a good performer. But now he sees the logic behind what I'm trying to accomplish, how it can help make government better, and therefore why it's something he should support. The more that leaders (both formal and informal) throughout the organization understand the underlying theory and purpose, the easier my job gets.

Structure of the MLDR

Much of the credit for the design and development of the MLDR goes to Kate Love-Jacobson (Manager, Professional Development and Quality Enhancement) and Deborah Munday (Coordinator, Professional Development and Quality Enhancement). They did a very thorough job:

"We did a lot of research, watched videotapes, reviewed books. We talked to other training professionals. We talked to the Total Quality Management Network staff about training and leadership issues. We attended other leadership training conferences so we could get some good ideas. We talked to other companies. We conferred with someone who does training for a local company.

"The roundtable is mostly about developing critical thinking skills. Also letting people know that the expectations in this new culture are that they can take risks, that mistakes are learning opportunities rather than opportunities to punish or embarrass. To let them know we have high expectations for them leading the charge. I think the learning organization culture is the foundation from which Lean and Six Sigma can sprout."

Kate Love-Jacobson (standing) and Deb Munday at an MLDR session.

The result is four days of training, spread out over 12 weeks. Each session has its own theme:

Day 1: Personal development and learning organization culture

Day 2: Leadership skills development

Day 3: Developing leadership in others

Day 4: Leadership tools

The sessions are very interactive, with a lot of exercises or projects to work on. In every session, people are divided into teams and receive assignments ranging from preparing an overview of a topic to performing an executive vignette (where they act out something that has to do with the topic for that session) to leading group activities. They work on these assignments between sessions.

The first roundtable class, which began in January 2004, consisted of hand-picked individuals that we saw as potential change agents. We were looking for positive, high-performing people who were charismatic and influential in their own way. The next few classes involved people recommended by department or division heads or by previous roundtable participants.

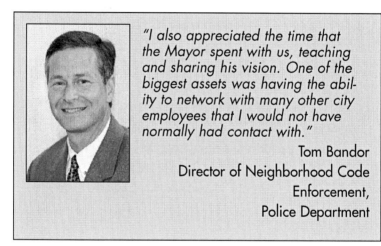

"I also appreciated the time that the Mayor spent with us, teaching and sharing his vision. One of the biggest assets was having the ability to network with many other city employees that I would not have normally had contact with."

Tom Bandor
Director of Neighborhood Code Enforcement,
Police Department

Numerous participants have told me that what they learned in the class has had a big impact on how they approach their work. For example, Mary Jane Slaton, who works in stakeholder relationships in our city utilities, recently commented that "It has totally changed how I think about projects. It's not just 'how is Mary Jane going to get this done?' but who else should be involved, how I should lead them, how I can use some of the skills I've learned to get other people on board." She went on to cite a current example of how she's putting her new understanding to work:

"Last year we finished constructing a wetland," she recalls. "One of the commitments we made to the community was to use the wetland for educational programs. Five years ago, I would have approached this with the mindset of 'get it done, keep it simple.' But through my new understanding of leadership, I knew this really needed to be a team effort. So I involved wetland protection groups, parks groups, and local land trust experts in the community because of their resources and background. We can benefit from having a whole team to help with curriculum development."

One of my favorite sayings is Warren Bennis's "none of us is as smart as all of us." Mary Jane confirms this conviction for me: "The other thing I took away was that the city has a huge number of resources. Many employees are bright and innovative, and if you're stuck on a problem or issue, you just need to tap into another employee. The MLDR was great for making connections with others. I learned not only what they do but also who they are as people and leaders. There are people in other departments whose insights

"My commitment [to improving neighborhoods] has been exclusively focused on effecting external changes that improve the lives and livelihood of Fort Wayne residents. I ignored any necessity to advocate change within the organization. The Mayor's Leadership Development Roundtable dissolved that ignorance by introducing me to the possibility and power of the Learning Organization."

Paul Spoelhof
Senior Planner, Community
Development Department

and perspectives I really appreciate. I can now call them for suggestions on how to deal with a number of different issues."

"My department is in charge of the planning and design of the city's water supply and waste water treatment, including everything engineering in between. We take our engineering and capital project management seriously, especially the responsibility of efficiently managing limited funding.

"What I really like about the Mayor's leadership programs is how I feel empowered to train our staff because of the Mayor's values and teaching about learning, training, and leadership. I am willing to go over budget in our training line item because I know that in the long run we are more effectively and efficiently managing our total engineering dollars and becoming less dependent on outside consulting engineering services. I believe in developing engineer learners. They appreciate the training.

"I also custom-designed a practical and purposeful mentorship program for our department. I always assign a senior leader to work with a less-experienced engineer.

"I've taken my department from 8 to 18 people. That might sound like a big jump, but we spend millions of dollars a year on engineering designs and contracts. Because of the training and mentoring, we're doing a better job of managing those projects and using more in-house resources."

Mark Gensic,
Manager, Planning Design Services, City Utilities

2. Managers as Champions and Sponsors

If you've studied the business model for Six Sigma, you know that there are two distinct roles for managers:

- At least one senior executive, called a **Champion**, serves as the representative of the initiative at the leadership level. Large companies may have multiple Champions (one at the corporate level, and one in each division), all with half- or full-time responsibilities for moving the Six Sigma initiative forward. In this model, the Champion's job is to plan and oversee deployment, make sure that appropriate resources are allocated to Six Sigma, and remove barriers at the corporate level. He or she has overall accountability for the results of the program.

- Local support for specific projects is provided by the manager who oversees the area where the project is occurring. This person is called the project **sponsor**. She or he has responsibility to support the project in all ways (such as making sure people have sufficient time and resources to complete the work, and making contact with people from other work areas or departments when issues cross organizational boundaries).

Using these definitions, I am the equivalent of the corporate-level Champion for Lean and Six Sigma efforts in Fort Wayne city government because the ultimate responsibility for success or failure rests with me. We also use the term Champion for department and division heads who are actively involved in rolling out Lean and Six Sigma efforts in their units, and for managers who are sponsors of a project. To us, the title isn't as important as the involvement.

"I viewed my job as the Champion of the IS/TO project [p. 111] as encouraging Dianne, the project leader, and keeping her momentum, getting rid of barriers, helping solve problems."

Sally Clem, Manager
Data Control Department [Public
Works and City Utilities]

The TQM Network that provides most of our Black Belt training also has a two-day Champion training that most city managers have now gone through. In other ways, success in getting managers involved has been mixed for a variety of reasons:

- For one thing, the fit between Six Sigma and needed improvements is more obvious in some operations than in others—because the processes are more visible, data collection opportunities more obvious, and the work relatively structured. That's one reason why you'll see more projects in this book from Public Works and City Utilities than, for example, from our safety functions such as Fire and Police.

- As shocking as it might sound, not everyone currently shares my passion for Lean and Six Sigma or for learning in general. And as I've mentioned before, given the lack of a mandate when I took office, it seemed best initially to let participation in these efforts be voluntary.

Even with these barriers, Lean and Six Sigma projects are becoming more widespread the more success stories we have to share. Employees at all levels can now look at many examples demonstrating that Lean and Six Sigma can make a positive difference and are applicable to their situations.

Challenges Still Remain

In this chapter, my intent was to give credit where credit is due and acknowledge the very impressive growth and leadership I've seen in many, many city employees. It is they who have convinced me that there is a pool of energy and enthusiasm for learning, growth, and leadership that lies untapped in your city, just as there was in mine.

Broader Impact

From all reports, the people who have really embraced leadership and have developed their skills are having a big impact in everyday life within the city government.

 Gina Kostoff, the Utilities Services Manager for the Board of Public Works, tells me that "The biggest thing I learned is that I need to tailor my management style and leadership style to the people I'm working with. I like to charge in and get the work done and move on. What I do works for me, but may not be the best way to motivate others. I learned I have to step back and be patient, listen, and learn how to motivate each individual.

"A leader is not just a manager," Gina continues. "Leadership doesn't belong to just one person. A good leader brings out good things, especially leadership skills, in other people. Empower and motivate people who work with you, then you can, as a team, charge in and accomplish anything."

That doesn't mean everyone has embraced the changes we're trying to introduce into the way that city government functions.

Kate Love-Jacobson, the head of our professional development efforts, points out that she regularly encounters "a lot of old management ideology, old behaviors that aren't really conducive to risk-taking." Her comment reflects the long history of adversarial relationships between management and non-management, and between transient political leaders and long-time city employees, including the strong unions that represent them.

Chet Shastri has seen these barriers firsthand. In the water treatment plant he oversees there was traditionally a clear split between operator duties and maintenance duties. "That meant operators never had to take ownership of the chemical feeding equipment. If maintenance didn't do something the way they like, the operators would complain," says Chet. Now, he continues, the group is adopting a Total Productive Maintenance (TPM) approach, where maintenance responsibilities are blended into everyday operations.

"That means the operators can adjust the equipment just the way they want to make their jobs easier," Chet says. But it also means they have more responsibilities and can't just point the finger at what is wrong with the machines.

The past is a place where taking risks was often punished, where going above and beyond your job description was discouraged, where there were no incentives to collaborate across organizational boundaries. We are trying to change those patterns in Fort Wayne, but we acknowledge that it takes a lot of hard work and "walking the talk" to change old mentalities.

Lessons Learned #3

While I knew from the beginning of my first term that I wanted to do something like the leadership roundtable, we lacked some critical capacity (see sidebar) and it never rose high enough on the priority list early on. But the outcome from the roundtable has been so positive to the overall effort that in retrospect we should have made a more urgent effort to launch it sooner.

The other change that we only recently made was to encourage all division and department heads go through the roundtable experience. Having more department lead-

Critical capacity: In-house HR

The human resource functions in Fort Wayne used to be contracted to an outside agency. That's fine as long as their main function is to process payroll and benefits. But it is not sufficient if you want your HR department to play a lead role in professional development and learning opportunities. We did establish an in-house HR department in January 2003. Now we get full service from HR, including additional management training (because a lot of employees have been promoted to management positions), helping departments with strategic planning, and running the MLDR.

ers aware of the need for a learning culture would also have helped ease the one negative effect we've seen: people come out of the sessions with a lot of energy and enthusiasm and high expectations for themselves... then return to their normal jobs, which are still ingrained in bureaucracy. Seeing the incongruity between old and new practices leaves them feeling deflated. We're fighting this deflation by sponsoring a monthly meeting for all MLDR alumni. But as Kate Love-Jacobson reminds me, "It's a tough hurdle. We're in the midst of changing the system we're sending them back to."

A third problem we recently recognized was that our leadership courses didn't incorporate any discussion of quality concepts. That meant we weren't preparing the people who went through the leadership course to support our quality efforts appropriately. We're in the process of changing that forced dichotomy by working to develop courses that cover both topics.

Conclusion

As noted in Chapter 1, through 2007, we have figures to show that Fort Wayne has generated over $13.5 million in savings and cost avoidance from our B.E.S.T. teams and Lean and Six Sigma efforts. That level of success in just five-and-a-half years tells me that a lot of people are taking on leadership roles at all levels of our organization.

On the other hand, when we look at projects that have not succeeded, it's clear the fault more often lies in a lack of leadership support than with an inadequacy on the part of the Black Belt or Green Belt. That tells me we aren't yet doing enough to get formal leaders excited about Lean and Six Sigma or excited about their role in picking good projects and providing the necessary support.

There's nothing more fulfilling as a mayor than to see people blossom professionally. And I'm fortunate to have more examples than space permits in this book. I never did believe the stereotypes of government workers, and now have abundant proof that the majority of people in city government are eager for opportunities to learn and expand their skills.

As one voice speaking one message about Lean and Six Sigma, my impact, even as Mayor, is limited. With dozens of voices around the city telling dozens of unique stories, the message has grown exponentially. People no longer have to take me at my word; they can listen to their colleagues and coworkers to get the real story about participating in the Leadership Roundtable, about taking Black Belt or Green Belt training, about what it feels like to lead a project and succeed. That is a very powerful force to drive change.

Featured Project #5

Quick & Lean

(Speeding up service requests in the Utilities department)

We didn't formally start using Lean techniques until early 2004 (see the next chapter for more details about Lean). This project happened in January 2005. I want to point out that the structure of this project is very different from typical Six Sigma projects (including those you've already read about in this book). We used a technique called Kaizen (ky-zen), where improvement happens via an intense workshop. In our version of Kaizen, people come together for a week, get trained in some basic Lean concepts and techniques, and work on their project in between training sessions. You'll find an outline of the Kaizen agenda on p. 152. The point is that most of what you'll read about here happened in a single week, and the project was completed the week after! It's that kind of rapid payback that makes this particular type of Lean project attractive to managers and staff alike. Dianne Bullard, a data control clerk, was one of the first participants in this new model and she did a stellar job.

"After being in the Lean project class that first day, the following day you don't know if you really want to go back," confesses Dianne Bullard. "It was very challenging. There was a lot of math. But both of the facilitators were very helpful during the week."

Background

Late in 2004, one of the staff in the Data Control department retired, followed by another retirement in February 2005. Greg Meszaros, the Director of City Utilities and Public Works, asked Sally Clem, the department manager, to see if the department processes could be improved with Lean tools to the point where she wouldn't need to hire any replacements. If the Lean analysis didn't generate any substantial gains, *then* he would sign off on refilling one of the positions. At the same time, Sally had been thinking that a portion of the work her department handled could be automated, and now seemed like the time to include that evaluation in the analysis. When the opportunity came along to send someone to Lean training and conduct a rapid-fire Kaizen project, she asked Dianne Bullard to take the lead. So Dianne spent a week in the Kaizen session, interacting frequently with Sally and her coworkers.

The data control operation receives and processes approximately 22,500 of what's called the "IS/TO read only" work orders each year. IS stands for "initiate service"; TO is "termination orders." "Read only" means the only service the city provides is reading the meter. Historically, the three data control clerks processed 90 work orders per day on average, which took about 14.4 hours a week to complete.

Team

Dianne Bullard, Howeda Stepp, Jeanne Bryers (Data Control Clerks) Don Clevenger (System Development Sr. Specialist); Heidi Williams (Work Order Clerk); Sally Clem (Dept. Mgr. / Champion) Maria Gomez Espino (Program Mgr./Co-facilitator); Lynn Clark (Facilitator); Len Poehler (City Utilities Controller); Greg Meszaros (Exec. Sponsor)

The Kaizen Event

Since our staff have little experience with Lean practices, the five-day improvement event combines both training and work on the process. Here's a quick overview:

Monday: Overview of Lean (7 forms of waste and various tools); review/refine project charters; map the "As Is" process; do the value-add/non-value-add analysis

Tuesday: Do baseline measurement collection, brainstorm what the process could be if waste (NVA) is eliminated, prepare project plan, review proposed changes with Champion

Wednesday: Define and implement changes, review with Champion if needed

Thursday: Prepare control plan, prepare and practice report-out presentation

Friday: Report out on the changes to team members, champion/department manager and executive management

Mapping the "as is" process means creating a flowchart that shows the steps in how the process currently works. The team discovered that—just as with the permitting process shown in Figure 14—the "before" process was complex and time consuming (involving 31 steps that required over 14 man-hours of processing).

Having a process map provides the foundation for Lean analysis for the second item listed on Monday, doing a value-add (VA) vs. non-value-add (NVA) analysis. Here's how Dianne describes that activity:

"The approach was to look at what we do, why we do it, and ask 'Is it necessary?'" she says. Deciding if something is necessary means determining if it contributes some essential feature or function to the process outcome, or is required for business or legal purposes (such as tracking budgets or ensuring compliance with statutes). Or, again in Dianne's words, "We needed to look at the time we spend and the cost to see if there's a way to eliminate waste and save time and money."

In her case, part of the solution was known prior to the Kaizen week: a shift to automated processing of the Initiate Service (IS) read-only requests. That move eliminated one entire subprocess. To make the shift, Dianne says she needed to work with Sally to get help from the Information Services department.

Other changes that arose during the week included centralizing a logging-in step. That eliminated the need for manual re-entry of various information into the billing system, and sped up the hand-off of orders to data control for processing. A decision was made to also automate processing of the 900+ "new sets" performed each year (the installation of a meter for the first time in a new home), reducing the cycle time from 5 minutes to about 3 minutes each.

Results

The automation and process changes let Sally's group...

- Cut process steps from 31 steps down to 17
- Save 374 man-hours for the IS/TO read-only process (50% lower than before) and 26 man-hours for a separate process (40% lower than before)—leading to more available time for staff to conduct other job-related duties (a savings of $7,500 per year in applied labor)
- Handle the lesser workload by the three existing staff, meaning the loss of one position did not harm customer service or quality—and saving $34,000/yr for that position
- Save $3,010 annually for supplies

What Made This Work

- **A little bit of courage.** As Dianne has herself confessed, this was the most math she'd done since high school a number of decades ago. And she's far from the only person in that position within city government. Being put in a position where you're unsure of success—and, worse still, unsure of your ability to succeed—is a new sensation for many city employees. I applaud Dianne's courage and determination.

- **And a lot of support.** Dianne says she got a lot of support during her Kaizen week. Her instructors were always available and willing to explain terms or help with the math; she often turned to her supervisor (Sally Clem), who stepped in to secure resources and cooperation from people in other departments.

Project leader Dianne Bullard (left) with her manager, Sally Clem.

There was resistance at first, says Sally Clem. People's reaction was "call it what you want, but this Lean stuff means you don't need my job any more." She says it was important not to show her frustration but to let them see that she was willing to make changes. She also helped allay fears by upgrading the skills of people in her department.

"As staff have become more cognizant, they've made recommendations on how to improve the work," says Sally. She set up an Ideas and Efficiencies Board outside her office where people could suggest improvements. For example, an employee came to Sally one day and showed her a report saying, "We get this report every day and just throw it away." They did a quick investigation and discovered that their department did a small portion of the report—just 3 pages out of the 120 pages generated daily. "No one had used this report before because they didn't realize there was important information in it," says Sally. "Now we're getting information we need and saving a few trees every day."

CHAPTER 5

Show Me the Data

What Six Sigma and Lean bring to the table

"I came to see that there are a lot of things you think you know. Sometimes you're right," says Mary Nelson-Janisse, the city Risk Manager during my first term. "But sometimes you're wrong. That's why it's good to have data to back up your decisions. There were a lot of things that surprised me. Data gives you a clearer picture."

Mary's comments capture one reason why data-based improvement approaches like Lean and Six Sigma have become so popular in the business world: They give you a clearer picture of what's really happening in the workplace so you can focus on the root cause of problems. That lets you figure out better ways to do your work and better ways to invest scarce resources.

If you've read the featured projects already presented, you'll have a good idea of what Six Sigma and Lean look like in practice—it's people who have new tools to investigate problems and develop better ways of getting their work done. Now let's look more closely at both of these disciplines.

Lean *and* Six Sigma — or Lean Six Sigma?

You may have noticed that sometimes I reference "Lean Six Sigma" and other times use "Lean and Six Sigma." There is a unified improvement discipline called Lean Six Sigma.

In our case, however, we ended up implementing the Six Sigma elements first, and only began the Lean side in 2004 (in hindsight, starting Lean sooner would have produced a more dynamic impact, as I'll discuss on p. 155). Hence, in practice, we did Lean and Six Sigma separately, and that's how they'll be covered in this chapter.

A Brief History Lesson

I pointed out in Chapter 3 that people who have come of age, in a business sense, in larger American companies probably have direct experience with at least some of the history of Lean Six Sigma. They appreciate its roots and why it's constructed the way it is. Since that knowledge is much rarer in government, I want to present a brief history. If you already know this Lean Six Sigma background, feel free to skip to the next section.

The origins of Six Sigma can be traced to the early parts of the 20th century when an American statistician named Walter Shewhart began studying variation, the major and minor fluctuations we see in any given process or sequence of tasks every single day. Think about the time it takes you to get to work, for example. It varies every day, right? Because there are a whole host of factors influencing just how long it takes on any given day, the difference in time is likely anywhere from a few minutes to a half-hour or more depending on how far you drive and the nature of the route.

If you wanted to minimize the amount of variation in your process—just like we want to minimize variation in our business processes—you'd need to apply Shewhart's theories to help you understand the patterns in the variation. Once you know what's contributing to the variation, you can develop strategies to eliminate or reduce the causes.

One of Shewhart's followers was a young engineer and mathematician named W. Edwards Deming, who got involved in the study of process and system improvement in the 1930s and '40s. Unfortunately for Deming, American businesses were doing so well after World War II that they paid little attention to his teachings. But across the Pacific Ocean he found a much more receptive audience—the Japanese, still reeling from the war years. In 1950, they invited Dr. Deming to teach them about variation and improvement. His visits gave rise to the original Total Quality Management (TQM) system, which focused on reducing variation and improving quality. He also influenced Taiichi Ohno, an employee of Toyota in the post-WWII years, who went on to develop the basis of the Toyota Production System (what we call Lean), which is built around the premise that any activities in the process that do not add value to the good or service are waste and should be eliminated.

It wasn't until 30 years later, in the early 1980s, that Deming found an audience in American businesses. Steep global competition and rising costs led many U.S. business leaders to embrace TQM principles and develop them even further.

While some companies had limited success with TQM projects, the investment in what was then known as "continuous improvement" didn't quite have the payback that companies had expected in terms of customer satisfaction, costs, quality, or speed. Projects would start but never finish. Nearly anyone could pick a project they wanted to work on, regardless of whether it had any links to business priorities. Education in improvement methods was spotty at best.

The way around these problems, people realized, was to:

1. **Develop a network** (or infrastructure) of people who would be dedicated to improvement work—making sure that results happened quickly and contributed to profits or cost savings. Specifically, companies started nominating a senior executive (usually called a Champion) who would represent "improvement" at senior levels—shaping the deployment, providing resources, and monitoring return on investment. They also began training a cadre of selected individuals who reported to the Champion, though deployed within a department or function. These latter roles were given names adopted from the martial arts (Black, Green, Yellow, and White Belts—see p. 186 for definitions).

2. Develop a **standard metric** for comparing process excellence. As mentioned in Chapter 1, that standard became known as **Six Sigma**, a name derived from the Greek symbol used to represent a certain amount of variation in a process.

- "Six" sigma represents an incredibly high standard of performance—only 3.4 defects out of every 1 million opportunities (or, more precisely, only 3.4 outputs out of every million will fall outside the specification limits for that process). Few processes actually operate at a six sigma level, but the term grew to embrace the whole improvement methodology.

Meanwhile, on the Lean front...

One thing that Toyota does better than any other company on Earth is operate quickly and efficiently. The company spent decades studying all the things that slow down a process—extra steps, too much inventory, too much movement, having to change machine settings—and developed specific methods for eliminating all those sources of waste.

When the TQM movement began taking off, American manufacturers also discovered the Toyota Production System, but at that time, that name wasn't very appealing, and the whole set of tools and methods for eliminating waste and improving process speed was renamed "lean manufacturing" in the U.S. It slowly but surely began to spread among production–based enterprises, but for about a decade or so was not recognized as something that could also be applied to service and transactional situations.

Melding the two disciplines

In the mid-1990s, companies began realizing that Lean and Six Sigma needed each other. Like the early days of TQM, Lean suffered because of the lack of infrastructure. Six Sigma was great at reducing defects and improving quality, but wasn't really suited to eliminating the waste that slowed processes down. The first true blending of the two disciplines came through my friend Mike George and his colleagues at George Group Consulting in Dallas, Texas. (You can read about the unified approach in his books *Lean Six Sigma* and *Lean Six Sigma for Service,* both published by McGraw-Hill.)

Yet the blending of these two approaches is still a relatively recent phenomenon, and the term Lean Six Sigma is not universally used. When doing your own research, look for anything labeled Six Sigma, Lean, or Lean Six Sigma.

You'll find details on how we trained people and filled the infrastructure requirement for Lean Six Sigma in Chapter 6. The remainder of this chapter will give a brief overview of the key concepts for each of these disciplines.

Basics of Six Sigma

Six Sigma is most often described as a process improvement methodology or structured problem-solving approach. Both are correct: it's a set of tools and concepts that help you dissect what's going on in a process, and pinpoint and eliminate the root causes of problems—which leads to sustainable improvement.

In this section, I want to highlight a few key concepts, focus on the data aspect of making decisions about improvement, then present the structured problem approach most often used with Six Sigma.

A. Key Concepts of Six Sigma

The entire framework of Six Sigma is built on just a handful of key concepts:

1. Work occurs through processes
2. Every process has customers
3. It's the customers who define quality
4. Decisions must be based on data
5. To achieve quality you have to control variation

1. Work occurs through processes

Adopting a process viewpoint simply means looking at work as a series of linked tasks rather than actions that occur independently. Words like "series" and "linked" are critical to Six Sigma thinking:

- They reflect the insight that work has a *flow*—and that we can create diagrams or maps of anything with a flow
- "Linked" means we need to understand what comes before the process we're studying and what happens afterwards

Figure 24 (next page), for example, is another example of a SIPOC-type of process map (see also Figure 10), which highlights Suppliers, the people or groups who provide Inputs to the Process, which in turn generates Output used by Customers.

Figure 24:
SIPOC Process map

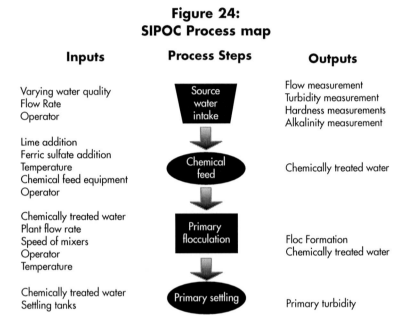

Inputs	Process Steps	Outputs
Varying water quality Flow Rate Operator	Source water intake	Flow measurement Turbidity measurement Hardness measurements Alkalinity measurement
Lime addition Ferric sulfate addition Temperature Chemical feed equipment Operator	Chemical feed	Chemically treated water
Chemically treated water Plant flow rate Speed of mixers Operator Temperature	Primary flocculation	Floc Formation Chemically treated water
Chemically treated water Settling tanks	Primary settling	Primary turbidity

This example of a SIPOC diagram comes from Vicki Zehr, the water quality supervisor at the Water Filtration Plant. It shows all the factors that can affect the primary turbidity level. The main process steps flowing down the center; inputs are on the left and outputs to the right.

Teams often create a map like this at the start of a project because it helps them...

- Define the boundaries of the project (the starting and endpoints of the process flow)
- Identify process factors (input and steps) that they'll likely want to study
- Develop metrics that will help them evaluate the

overall process health (a measure linked to one of the key outputs)

2. Every process has customers

The whole point of a process is to produce the outputs that somebody, somewhere needs for *their* job. These "somebodies" are the **customers** of the process. They can be either inside or outside the organization.

Understanding and reconciling the needs of various customers is a key component of Six Sigma projects. Featured Project #3 (p. 51., for example, related the experience of Heather Presley, the Deputy Director of Community

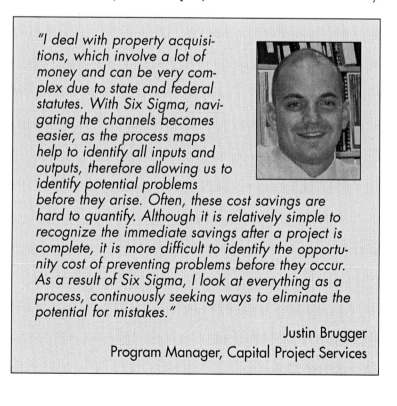

"I deal with property acquisitions, which involve a lot of money and can be very complex due to state and federal statutes. With Six Sigma, navigating the channels becomes easier, as the process maps help to identify all inputs and outputs, therefore allowing us to identify potential problems before they arise. Often, these cost savings are hard to quantify. Although it is relatively simple to recognize the immediate savings after a project is complete, it is more difficult to identify the opportunity cost of preventing problems before they occur. As a result of Six Sigma, I look at everything as a process, continuously seeking ways to eliminate the potential for mistakes."

Justin Brugger
Program Manager, Capital Project Services

Development for Housing, who led a project to reduce the time it takes to review and approve land improvement permits. It was a classic government problem where different customers have seemingly opposite needs:

- Developers want quick approval ("fast cycle time" in Six Sigma terms)
- Citizens want quality developments that don't contribute to problems like traffic and drainage

Balancing these needs is why society imposes a review on the permitting process. Heather's challenge: to develop a process that met both customers' needs. She and her team managed to do it.

We all have customers

Because few city departments are directly involved in selling goods or services, there is a tendency for many government employees to think they don't have customers.

As I hope this discussion makes clear, anyone who works in a process (and we all do) has customers. They are the people who use the output from your work.

---

3. It's customers who define quality

Traditionally, people working on a process have taken all their direction from their supervisors or managers. Only those people in positions of authority had the power to establish and enforce requirements for the work. Only they could officially judge work as acceptable or not. So only their "voice" mattered.

In the past two decades it has become clearer that this kind of internal focus leads to unhappy customers and a lot of waste along the way. In the end, the customers of a process are the final and most important arbiters of quality. They are the people who will decide if we've done a good job. So it is the "voice of the customer" (in Six Sigma lingo) that we need to listen to.

A project in our police department, for example, discovered that robbery victims cared most about knowing what was happening with their cases. Simply being contacted by the police department within a few days of the crime and being told the status—even if the outcome was that the case was unsolvable—was in some ways more important to them than solving the crime itself.

Over at the fire department, Battalion Chief Kenn Kunze took on a project to improve the patient charts for EMS runs. Some of the customers and needs he identified were:

Customer	Need
Patient	Better patient care
Hospital	Complete, accurate chart
Fire Dept:	Reduced criminal and civil liability
	Increased trust and respect of cooperative agencies and Medical Director
	Maintain State of Indiana Provider Certification
	Save time (1 hour per report) 202 hrs/year

Understanding these needs allowed him to define improvement targets for his project.

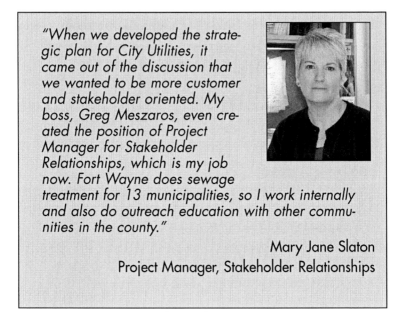

"When we developed the strategic plan for City Utilities, it came out of the discussion that we wanted to be more customer and stakeholder oriented. My boss, Greg Meszaros, even created the position of Project Manager for Stakeholder Relationships, which is my job now. Fort Wayne does sewage treatment for 13 municipalities, so I work internally and also do outreach education with other communities in the county."

Mary Jane Slaton
Project Manager, Stakeholder Relationships

4. Decisions must be made on data

At the beginning of this chapter I quoted our former risk manager (Mary Nelson-Janisse) describing why she's come to rely on data. The fact is that data-based decision making was foreign to most people in Fort Wayne city government six years ago. But, like Mary, once people see the value of data collection and analysis, they never want to go back. Data analysis becomes the way they do business, both inside and outside formal improvement projects. And you don't have to take my word for it:

- Phil GiaQuinta, Utilities Services Manager, says, "What I liked most about Six Sigma was that it eliminated our reliance on opinions and emotional responses to problems. You get rid of the 'I *think*' and really zero in on what's causing the problems." Even more important, he adds, is having the ability to tell whether something  really is a problem. "Now when people want to change something, I always ask 'What's the impact? What's your evidence that there's a problem? If there's not going to be that much of an impact, why bother fixing it?" says Phil.

- Patrick Ray, our former webmaster said, "I like that Six Sigma forces you to look at the data instead of relying on how you feel about your process. In the beginning of my project, I felt like the defects were much more widespread than they turned out to be. The data showed me that I could probably make more of an impact working on a different problem or process because the one I selected wasn't as bad as I thought initially."

- "What has happened is that I've started asking more questions that someone needs to substantiate with data," says Chet Shastri, Superintendent of the Water Filtration Plant. Most times, he says, "what I think" is not acceptable unless it's an emergency. "People have learned that they have to come to me with data. It's tough—some people are good at that, but some people still don't see the need for data. And some people are afraid of using tools because they don't want to take the time. But we've started doing things like evaluating the effectiveness of our analyzers using Six Sigma tools."

- "The use of data has completely reshaped what purchasing means now compared to 10 years ago," says our Director of Purchasing, Jim Howard. "We're much more focused on the total cost of ownership," he says. "For example, we have a matrix that helps us evaluate different vehicles, their  performance, and warranties." Data also appears in a lot of smaller purchasing decisions, continues Jim. "Data showed us that we weren't getting any bang for the buck by requiring competitive bids for anything under $5,000." As a result, people no longer have to get competing bids for purchases below that limit (the only requirement is that they seek minority suppliers whenever possible). The change in limit has saved a lot of time in the purchasing process.

5. To achieve quality you have to control variation

Think about any process you perform regularly—driving to work, writing a report, making a widget, calling customers. Undoubtedly there is variation in that process because nothing happens exactly the same way every day. Sometimes you run into heavy traffic on your drive in, sometimes you hit road construction, sometimes the weather slows you down.

Figure 25 shows data from a project led by Pat Faherty (Manager of Meter Reading), who worked on increasing the number of water meters his staff could read in one hour (above and beyond the gains we got from switching to automated reading systems).

Figure 25:
Dotplot of Number of Meters Read Per Hour

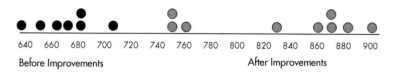

Before Improvements   After Improvements

> Displaying data in a dotplot is an easy way to get a visual picture of what the data look like. Here, 17 data points are spread out, ranging from 640 to 900 meters read per hour. That's variation. This chart was created after Pat's project was complete, and as you can see there is no overlap between the before and after numbers—showing that you don't need sophisticated charts to demonstrate project gains!

Pat Faherty (left) and meter-reading staff Ruben Alvarez, Herb Banks (in vehicle) and Don Miller.

One of Walter Shewhart's great insights that has endured to this day is that we don't have to just accept the variation in our processes. We can, in fact, isolate the causes of at least some of the variation and remove them from the process—thereby making our processes more predictable and better able to *reliably* deliver what customers want. The details of understanding and attacking variation are beyond the scope of this book, but be aware it's a topic you'll study a lot if you take Six Sigma training.

B. Learning From Data: The value of visual displays

It is true that Six Sigma involves data and some statistics. And yes, you'll need a trained statistician or Master Black Belt (at least initially) to teach you the basics and perform some of the data analyses. But what I like about Six Sigma tools is that they make it easy to learn from data in ways that a table of numbers never affords. Better yet, you don't have to be a statistician to interpret them. Here are just a few tools to prove this point to you.

Pareto Chart

A Pareto chart is a specialized bar chart that provides **focus** to a project. It depicts data on the frequency or impact of different elements of a problem. There is often a clear pattern showing that just a few elements are causing most of the problem—meaning that's where you should focus your improvement effort because that's where you'll get the biggest payback.

Variation relative to specifications defines the "sigma" level

When people speak of sigma in a generic sense, they're referring to how much variation there is in a process relative to how much is acceptable to customers. The concept is shown graphically in Figure 26. As you can see, in a typical process, a lot of output falls outside what customers find acceptable. Those "customer expectation limits" (called specification limits in manufacturing) can relate to anything—such as how long it takes to deliver a service or product, or how many errors they'll accept. In a process that operates at a "six sigma" level (lower part of the graph), all of the process output is well within customer expectations.

Figure 26: Process output vs. specifications

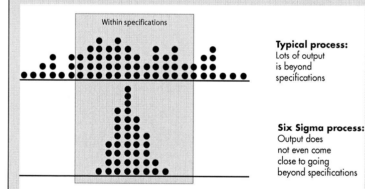

Within specifications

Typical process:
Lots of output is beyond specifications

Six Sigma process:
Output does not even come close to going beyond specifications

The "sigma" level of a process indicates how likely it is that the process output will be unacceptable to customers ("beyond specifications"). In a true "six" sigma process, the chances are extremely rare (only 3.4 times per million).

Katherine Pargmann in our Parks and Recreation Department, for example, was trying to reduce the number of unnecessary calls in the forestry division about tree trimming. She and her team collected data on the types of calls (noting the reasons for each call) and created the Pareto chart shown in Figure 27. Even if you've never seen a chart like this before, where would you suggest she concentrate her efforts? I'd pick the three tallest bars to the far left.

Figure 27:
Pareto Chart

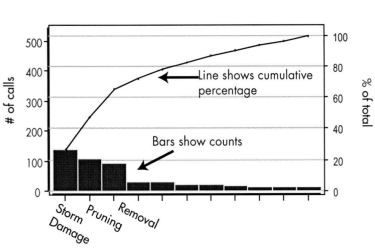

This Pareto chart summarizes data collected on the reasons for calls to the forestry division.

"By collecting baseline data on forestry calls and then reviewing the subsequent Pareto charts," says Kathy, "it provided a focal point for the project. I was then able to focus on the heavy hitters with the most impact."

Project leader Katherine Pargmann and members of the tree trimming crew, from L to R, Chad Tinkel, Dean Cook, Steve Goodwin, Adam Fluent, and John Chavez.

Mini-Case: Using Pareto charts

Jim Howard, our Director of Purchasing, says his department has been using Pareto charts to help understand city spending habits and where the big bucks are spent. One of the big bars on a Pareto chart was money spent on consulting services. Going down another layer, they discovered that a big chunk of that money was spent paying external engineering services for laying water mains. "We had a lot of history there we could review, and saw that there was a lot variation in how we spent. We launched a project to investigate what drove the costs and figured out we could predict the engineering costs pretty closely based on the length of the water main that was being replaced. It turned out that a lot of the things we thought were affecting costs weren't. This predictive model allows us not only to estimate our costs better but also to evaluate bids."

Time plot

One of the simplest ways to chart process data is to plot the points in time order. The resulting **time plot** is useful both for studying the causes of problems (see, for example, the Figure 23 on p. 90) and for tracking progress, as shown in Figure 28. That time plot is from a project led by Phil GiaQuinta, who was working to reduce the amount of time that customers calling his department had to wait on hold. Again, it's easy to see a pattern even if you're not familiar with this type of chart. The wait times dropped dramatically as a result of the project and have stayed low.

Figure 28:
Time Plot of Call Wait Times

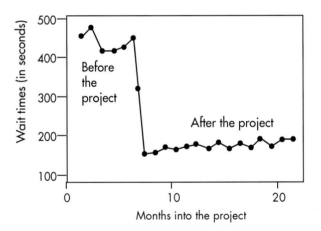

A time plot displays data points in the order in which they were collected. Here, the data points represent how long callers had to wait on hold before talking to a staff member. Even this kind of simple plot effectively demonstrates how much progress was made in the project.

Control chart

As I discussed earlier, one of the biggest advances in improvement was Walter Shewhart's work on understanding the patterns caused by variation and what those patterns tell us about the types of changes needed to improve process performance. Variation in time-ordered data is usually studied through the use of **control charts** like the one shown in Figure 29, taken from the robbery case disposition project.

Figure 29:
Control Chart of Robbery Case Disposition Time

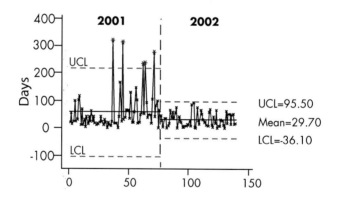

The figure shows the data points in the order in which they were collected (much like the previous time plot), but with some additional lines:

- The **average** (or "arithmetic mean")
- Upper and lower **control limits** that tell you how much variation is expected in the process

What do you notice about the two halves of this chart? For one thing, the control limits are much closer together in the "after" section. That's a really good thing. In statistical terms, it means the process is much more reliable now. More important, in people terms it means that almost all robbery victims hear about the disposition of their cases within about 30 days on average (with rare instances of two or three times that long). Look at the labeled points in the "before" section of the chart—those points mean that many people had to wait nearly a year before there was any resolution to their cases.

Capability analysis

Earlier, I talked about how "six sigma" in the statistical sense is a way to gauge process performance against customer needs or expectations. A **capability analysis chart** is another way to do this. For example, Figure 30 shows another chart from Phil GiaQuinta's call wait time project.

Figure 30: Visual Depiction of Process Capability

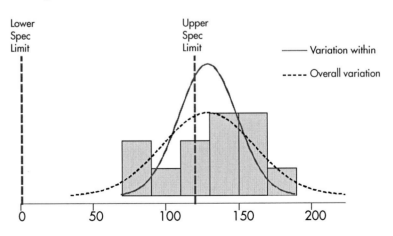

Again, even without any statistical training, it's pretty easy to see that a lot of the data falls *outside* or beyond the upper specification limit (labeled USL on the chart)—that means the calls are taking longer to answer than customers would like. A lot of people prefer graphs like these to the calculation of a "sigma" number because the charts give them a picture of the problem that is easier to translate into practical terms.

B. The DMAIC Improvement Structure

Another key aspect of Six Sigma is that it incorporates a standard problem-solving process known by the acronym DMAIC (duh-MAY-ick). The letters stand for the five phases:

DEFINE the goals and boundaries for the project based on customer and business need

MEASURE the problem (gather data)

ANALYZE the data and interpret data charts to pinpoint the most likely causes of the problem

IMPROVE the problem by defining, testing, and implementing solutions targeted at the confirmed causes

CONTROL the process going forward to make sure the gains are maintained

The beauty of approaches like DMAIC is the logic and discipline they impose on the problem solver:

- You don't gather data until you've defined specifically what you want to measure

- You only get to solutions *after* you've gathered and analyzed data—so the improvements you implement will be based on facts, not gut feelings or intuition

- The danger of backsliding (a common occurrence with other improvement methods) is lessened because of the Control step, which requires you to document the new methods or procedures, train everyone involved in the process on the new methods, and establish data collection procedures to monitor performance into the future

(All of the Six Sigma projects featured in this book followed the DMAIC structure, though we haven't labeled the DMAIC phases in the project descriptions. You can find full project reports at www.performanceisthebestpolitics.com.)

"In our case, the problem wasn't defining the problem," says Phil GiaQuinta. *"You don't need to do a survey to know that people don't like standing in line or being put on hold. But data helped us understand exactly how to go about fixing those problems."*

Basics of Lean

The primary goal of Lean is to remove waste from a process. What do we mean by waste? It includes:

- Delays
- Excess motion
- Excess transportation (carrying reports up and down stairs, moving spare parts around a warehouse)
- Inventory that is not going to be used immediately (as Rick Orr's street light inventory project makes clear, excess inventory just ties up funds that could be put to good use elsewhere; see Featured Project #6, p. 163)
- Doing something that no customer wants

Deciding what is waste and what isn't, and acting appropriately, form the key concepts of Lean.

Key Lean Concepts

Three Lean concepts that have proved particularly useful to us are:

1. The need to distinguish between value-added (VA) and non-value-added (NVA) work
2. Looking for waste in all its forms
3. The speed advantage lies in getting rid of NVA work (waste)

Lean Concept #1: Distinguish between value-added and non-value-added work

Put yourself in your customer's shoes then look back at your own process. Does every step in that process contribute to the result that you (the customer) want? If you were being billed separately for every step, would you be willing to pay for all of them?

The answer to both questions, in the vast majority of cases, will be "no." A lot of work in processes does not add value—and it's that work that Lean tries to eliminate. Hence the key concept of Lean is to distinguish between value-added (VA) and non-value-added (NVA) work. In fact, analyzing process steps and categorizing each as VA or NVA is one of the first activities you'll do in most Lean projects.

"Required" NVA

Lean tools focus on eliminating NVA work in all its forms. However, the distinction between VA and NVA gets a little murky in some circumstances.

Traditionally, the label of VA is reserved for work that contributes to what customers want from a process. However, some of the remaining NVA work is required for legal or regulatory purposes—it adds value in the sense of keeping us in compliance, but is waste in the customer's eyes. Since we can't eliminate this "required" waste, it is not usually a target for improvement and is often labeled separately from other kinds of NVA work.

Lean Concept #2: Look for waste (NVA) in all its forms

The Lean methodology evolved in manufacturing settings, where waste is often staring you in the face. It's easy to see waste when it's represented by piles of inventory or huge bins of partially completed assemblies stacked on a warehouse floor. We have a few such places: the smaller piles of street lighting components, for example, is a clear visual symbol of our progress in reducing that inventory.

But much government work is transactional in nature. And waste is either very hard to see in a transactional process or is often just accepted as the way the process works. So part of becoming a Lean enterprise means learning to identify waste in all its forms. Here are six of them:

1. *Waiting/delays.* If your customers could have their way, their requests for service would be filled instantaneously. Instead, in most processes, items of work sit around for long periods of time before the "value-added" work is performed. How long does it take for people in your departments to review building permits? To repair a pothole? To fix a burned-out streetlight? Wait times or delays are prime targets for elimination with Lean methods.

2. *Excess Inventory* is the accumulation of anything—materials, requests, orders, components, forms, supplies—beyond what is immediately needed to perform the tasks at hand. That may sound overly strict—after all, most of us feel comfortable with a pile of work waiting for our attention, or a large stockpile of parts (so we

know we'll never run out when we need something). But excess physical inventory represents a waste of money (see the street light inventory project on p. 163) and a waste of space, not to mention the potential that the materials will degrade before being used. An inventory of paperwork means that customers are suffering long delays (see item #1 in this list). Either way, if you find places in a process where work stacks up, use that clue to help focus your Lean improvement efforts.

3. ***Overproduction*** and 4. ***Overprocessing*** are sometimes confused: Overproduction is producing more output than is immediately needed by customers. Overprocessing (which they call "processing excessively" in Fort Wayne) is putting more effort into a work item than is needed or wanted by customers. In government work, overproduction might mean printing more hand-books or flyers than we could use in a month or two. Overprocessing might be printing those flyers as glossy four-color pieces when customers would be happy with a one-color brochure. Overprocessing can also take the form of redundancy—having a permit reviewed by 10 people, for example, when only 2 or 3 are adding value to the process. The arguments against these "overs" are the same: in both cases, you're wasting time and money that could be better spent on other priorities.

5. ***Excess Transportation*** is moving materials around with-out adding any value to them. In his book *Lean Six Sigma for Service*, Mike George cites a banking process where one type of deposit transaction traveled more than three miles in physical distance within a single office build-ing—simply from the cumulative effect of being sent up and down stairs and to various different offices as the

transaction traveled back and forth between functions. A little physical rearrangement of the office space (and elimination of wasted steps) reduced that distance to something like 400 feet. In manufacturing operations, excess transportation more often takes the form of shuffling around inventory or work-in-process—material is constantly being moved into new spaces or locations, often for little purpose other than to make space for other inventory.

6. *Excess Motion* is any movement by process operators (the people actually doing the tasks) beyond the minimum necessary to perform the VA work. For example, many times the supplies or information needed to perform a job is not within arm's reach. So the operators have to move around, maybe even leave their workstations, to retrieve forms, envelopes, stamps, a report—whatever they are lacking. Or they have to stretch uncomfortably to get something that could easily be moved within reach. The application of efficient and ergonomic motion principles is more apparent in manufacturing or production environments, but more and more transactional functions are recognizing the value in having a well-organized workspace that minimizes physical discomfort.

The seventh form of waste: Defects

There is a seventh form of waste usually included in this list: defects. A defect is anything that is not done right the first time or to your customers' expectations. As a result, the process operators must either scrap the work item or rework it in some way—or run the risk of dissatisfying the customers. An invoice with an incorrect billing address will cause rework once it is returned and someone must search for the correct address then resend the invoice. I did not include defects with the other forms of waste listed here because finding and preventing defects is more often considered the domain of Six Sigma than of Lean.

Adding defects to the list, however, has led to a new acronym used in City Utilities and Public Works that helps them remember these forms of waste: DOTWIMP (for defects, overproduction, transportation, waste, inventory, motion, processes excessively).

Lean Concept #3: The speed advantage lies in getting rid of NVA work (waste)

Suppose I gave you a stopwatch and asked you to measure the amount of VA time in one of your processes. Then I asked you to measure total process time—how long it takes any item in the process (phone call, report, batch of waste water, pothole complaint) to travel through the entire process.

What percentage of time do you think is spent on VA work? The answer stuns most people. In world-class companies, VA work is usually only 20% to 25% of the total process time. In typical manufacturing processes, the figure is more like 10%. And in typical transactional processes (like most government work), it falls to less than 5%.

So here's a "Lean 101" question: Do you think you'll gain more speed by getting really, really fast at the VA work, or by eliminating the NVA work? The answer, of course, is to eliminate the waste.

The link between speed and waste

One way to state the goal of Lean efforts is to eliminate waste, but you could also say it is to maximize process speed, because those statements mean the same thing. For example, if someone processing customer service requests has stack of requests (the "waste" of inventory), it will take a long time to process the next request that comes in. Or think about how much longer it would take to approve a permit request that has to be reviewed by five different offices (the waste of transportation and overprocessing) than a request handled by one person. Or consider two citizen complaints that come into my office: one transcribed correctly and the other with errors (meaning we have to recontact the person making the complaint—the waste of defects). It's obvious which will be handled more quickly.

In most processes, much more time is spent on activities that you'll soon view as waste than on those your customers would consider as value-added work. So if you want to achieve speed, you have to get rid of the waste.

Sample Lean tools

Value Analysis (VA/NVA) flowchart

Often the simplest way to plunge into Lean analysis is to ask your process staff to first develop a flowchart of a work process, then identify which steps are valued by customers (VA) and which aren't (NVA)—as shown in Figure 31. Then challenge them to find ways to eliminate as much of the NVA work as possible.

Figure 31: VA/NVA flowchart

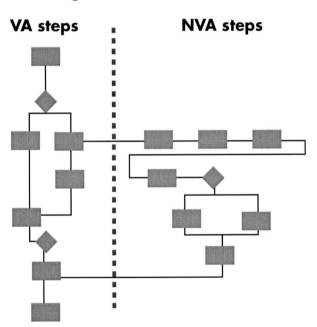

In this flowchart, the left side shows value-added steps, the right side shows non-value-added work. Another way to accomplish the same goal is to circle or color code steps on a regular flowchart.

Value-stream map

A value stream map (VSM) is simply a flowchart with data—specifically, data on time and "inventory" (any physical or virtual stack of inputs or partially completed work items). Both kinds of data are critical to effective Lean work. Knowing where time is wasted in a process is *the* key to improving process speed. Finding inventory and work-in-process (partially completed work items) indicates that something inefficient is going on.

Figure 32: Format of a Value-Stream Map

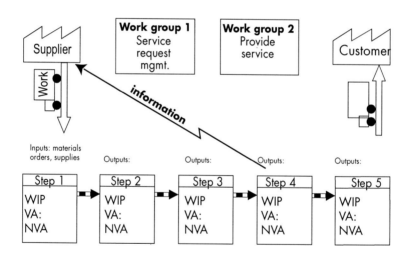

This schematic shows the basic elements of a value-stream map. You can see that there are process steps like in a regular flowchart. What's different is that you also need to enter data on WIP (the amount of "working process" at each step) and time (divided into VA and NVA segments). Traditionally, the flow of materials and information is also included.

Kaizen: The Lean Improvement Method

Lean problems *can* be tackled through the DMAIC structure discussed above (i.e., teams can use any Lean tool as appropriate during a project). But often the preferred path is to hold what's called a Kaizen (ky-zen) session. Kaizens are intense, usually one-week improvement sessions where participants focus only on their targeted improvement. The standard structure for our Kaizens is:

Monday
> Training
> Charter review / refine
> Map "As Is" process
> VA/NVA analysis

Tuesday
> Baseline measurement collection
> Value-Added / Non-Value-Added evaluation
> Brainstorm future state

Wednesday
> Develop changes
> Review changes with Champion

Thursday
> Prepare control plan
> Draft report

Friday
> Finish report
> Management presentation

Maria Gomez-Espino (standing) leads a session during a Lean Kaizen week. Shown here (L to R) are Mike Woods, Heidi Williams, Phil Boykin, Norb Nagel, and Nathaniel Edwards. Not shown but on the team are Jerome Schoenle, Len Poehler, and Cindy Huss.

This focused structure has many benefits but also brings some limitations:

> **Benefit:** Improvements happen quickly—often within the Kaizen week or soon thereafter (if follow up on details is needed).

> **Limitations:** Obviously, you can't use this method to solve a problem if it takes days or weeks to gather the needed data.

> **Best uses:** Excellent for solving process flow/process waste problems because it's relatively easy to map most processes and find opportunities for improvement. *Can* be used for more traditional Six Sigma problems if the data cycles are short enough.

Broader uses for Kaizens

Holding dedicated sessions around a well-focused issue or problem has much broader application than Lean projects. Some companies are using them at the start of innovation projects to speed up the development cycle. You can also use them to speed up portions of a traditional Six Sigma project: At Lockheed Martin, for example, a team leader and a facilitator sometimes hold a quick team meeting to scope the problem, go offline to collect data, and then come back for a one- or two-day Kaizen session with the full team to analyze that data and develop solutions.

> "Six Sigma taught me to be more focused as a manager," says Phil GiaQuinta. "Sometimes you can start going in all directions. Six Sigma helps you focus on those top two or three things that are really why you're here in the first place."

Lessons Learned #4

Having worked with Six Sigma for more than five years and with Lean for more than a year, we've made our share of mistakes along the way. Two lessons jump out:

1. We should have incorporated Lean methods sooner
2. We could have emphasized the managerial-level use of data

1. We should have incorporated Lean methods sooner

Though Lean and Six Sigma share a common goal of making processes run faster and better, recall that the two disciplines evolved independently and thus approach that goal from different angles:

- Six Sigma tools are best for identifying the underlying cause of "defects" in a process, product, or service, such as getting wrong answers when calling for information or having a trash pickup missed. The prescriptive five-step DMAIC method is great for defining when and where defects occur, what's causing them, and how to eliminate those causes. The primary outcome of Six Sigma projects is gains in quality; any gains in speed are usually incidental.

- Lean tools, in contrast, focus on getting rid of anything that slows down a process without adding to the value of the product or service being delivered. There is no prescriptive approach, though most Lean efforts start by mapping a process and tracking how all the pieces of the process fit together: how the work flows from one step to another, where information and materials enter, where the work piles up, how long it takes to go from one step to another. That analysis leads to different ways to restructure the process to eliminate the biggest causes of delays.

During the first four years of the effort in Fort Wayne, our training and projects dealt solely with Six Sigma. We didn't start doing Lean training until 2004. In retrospect, we were living that old adage, "If all you've got is a hammer, every problem looks like nail." We have a list of Six Sigma projects that stalled out or didn't work at all. We now realize that some of them didn't require a full-blown DMAIC approach (perhaps a few simple tools would have sufficed) and many others would have been better handled with the tools of Lean:

- Lean tools work especially well in administrative and transactional situations because many processes are inefficient. Simply cleaning up the process flow has led to significant improvement in many areas.

- Lean tools focus on how a process currently works, which everybody has opinions about! In contrast, Six Sigma methods require people to collect and analyze data, which is foreign to many employees. We've found that people who first work on a Lean project gain confidence that allows them to tackle Six Sigma-type projects more readily. A little exposure through Lean leads to a devotion to data-based decision making.

- In part because we were limited by our lack of full-time Black Belts, many Six Sigma projects lasted well over a year—much of that time spent figuring out what kind of data to collect, then collecting and analyzing it. We don't begrudge that effort because the data is necessary to making true, lasting improvement in some problems. But we've found that we have low-hanging fruit when it comes to Lean methods— meaning that with Lean tools we can generate major improvements in time and costs in a week (if we use the Kaizen approach), or in a month or two at most.

Overall, we're finding that the Lean approach is gaining quicker acceptance because of the short cycle time and immediacy of results. We'd strongly recommend that you incorporate Lean techniques early on in your own deployment.

At the same time, we don't want to fall into the "hammer" trap. We're in the process of setting up teams of people who will review the various problems that people want to tackle and determine which method or tool is best suited for each situation. You may benefit from something similar.

2. We could have emphasized managerial-level use of data

All decisions are better when informed with data, not just those made during an improvement project. That theme is so central to our ability to achieve excellence that now we're talking about how we can create better awareness of the need for data-based decision making, especially at the executive levels, because that's the best way to model data use for the entire organization. We want to do more on two fronts in particular:

A) Asking for data

Let's say I asked our top 20 division heads and department leaders, "What measurements do you look at every day to make sure your department is improving?" Some could answer off the top of their heads. But others would have to spend maybe a day or more getting an answer.

That tells me we haven't yet reached the point where an appreciation for data is embedded into our culture. Any senior executive ought to be able to ask questions like, "What measurements do you look at once a week or more to judge whether you are reaching your goals? What is your measurement system? How do you know you are getting better?"

There's an old business saw that states "what gets measured, gets done." That's true because what we choose to measure reflects our priorities.

B) Using executive-level metrics to monitor overall results

Creating a workplace that highly values data is slow work, in part because at first only people who participate on projects get exposed to the benefits of a more data-driven life. I will admit to constantly bombarding managers with the "how do you know you're improving" question, but we still need to do more organization-wide to drive the use of data, especially at the managerial and executive levels.

To address this gap, we're emphasizing more and more that managers at all levels need to review data to monitor how their work unit is doing. Greg Meszaros is one of the leaders in this area (see sidebar, next page) though we're not yet where we should be.

What I would like to see are actual **dashboards**, which are physical displays of key metrics with some indication of the goal. Had we established a citywide dashboard early on, and required a similar dashboard at the division level, there would have been a greater awareness of the need for data and performance metrics as a way to evaluate progress (or

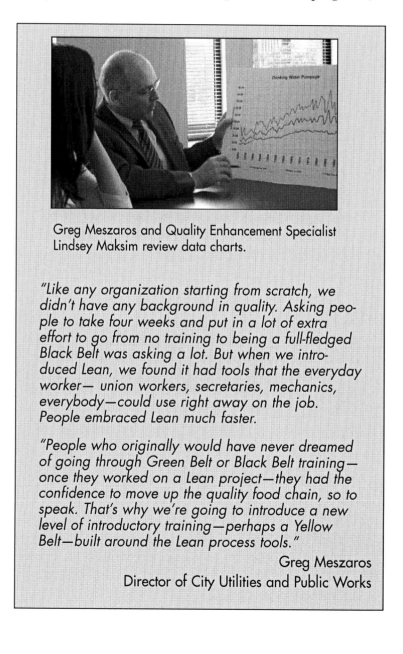

Greg Meszaros and Quality Enhancement Specialist Lindsey Maksim review data charts.

"Like any organization starting from scratch, we didn't have any background in quality. Asking people to take four weeks and put in a lot of extra effort to go from no training to being a full-fledged Black Belt was asking a lot. But when we introduced Lean, we found it had tools that the everyday worker— union workers, secretaries, mechanics, everybody—could use right away on the job. People embraced Lean much faster.

"People who originally would have never dreamed of going through Green Belt or Black Belt training— once they worked on a Lean project—they had the confidence to move up the quality food chain, so to speak. That's why we're going to introduce a new level of introductory training—perhaps a Yellow Belt—built around the Lean process tools."

Greg Meszaros
Director of City Utilities and Public Works

the lack thereof). Also, using standard metrics across all divisions would help people more accurately judge progress across the city as a whole.

Figure 33:
Dashboard Schematic

Just like the real thing, a "managerial" dashboard visually displays the status of key gauges. Typically, these will include an important time metric, something related to customers, and other quality goals.

Conclusion

In talking with dozens of city employees, I know that most had no idea what the terms "Six Sigma" or "Lean" meant before they got involved themselves. That unfamiliarity alone led to some anxiety, which grew further when they discovered they would have to work with data and even do some math. But now, after the fact, they are universally supportive of the need to teach people these skills. They've come to appreciate that:

1. Six Sigma and Lean aren't just a set of data tools. They represent a whole framework for how to approach improvement. The *logic* they impose on problem solving is as important as any of the individual tools.

2) You don't need a degree in statistics to effectively use Lean and Six Sigma methods. Yes, there is some analysis involved, but that's why you'll have internal or external coaches to help you out. Most of the tools are easy to interpret with minimal training—and you'll get a lot of bang with very little investment.

I hope you noticed that the results from all the projects have been maintained anywhere from months (for projects that were completed in 2004) to years (from the earliest projects done in 2000). These projects demonstrate why Lean and Six Sigma results are sustainable:

- Teams of people who "touch" the problem in some way and represent different perspectives are brought together; having these people all looking at the same problem at the same time is critical to process improvement

- Team leadership is strengthened by giving people the skills, tools, and structures they need to be successful

- People develop a clear outcome-based definition of a problem, meaning they describe the impact of a problem and what different result is needed to better serve the community; this clarity of purpose makes sure that everyone is on the same page about the importance of solving the problem

- The focus is on identifying problems that occur in a process, not placing blame on individuals

- Data is required for everything: from defining the severity of a problem to establishing baseline performance levels, deciding what solutions to try, and evaluating the end results

- People are forced to dig for root causes of problems and generate solutions for those specific root causes (rather than taking generic actions that don't affect the root causes)

Featured Project # 6

Overstock

Tackling street light inventory

As you probably know, Six Sigma is an improvement method shaped around data-based decision making. Trouble is, a lot of times the data don't exist, so you've first got to set up a system for collecting data. City Utilities Finance Manager Rick Orr did an excellent job of this in a project to reduce inventory in the street lights operation, which to date has freed up more than $500,000 for use elsewhere.

"When people heard that I was working on reducing inventory, they were concerned that that would harm city operations," says Rick Orr. "That's not the case at all. Inventory control is a matter of using resources wisely. You don't want a lot of money tied up in stacks of material that are just sitting around gathering dust."

Background

Early in 2003, Greg Meszaros (by then the Director of Public Works and City Utilities) told Rick Orr (City Utilities Finance Manager) that he thought there might be a problem with inventory in the street lights division. But there wasn't any data. And other people disagreed: "The guys who had worked there for years and years had their own perceptions," Rick remembers. "They weren't convinced there was a problem. I had no prior knowledge of street light inventory, so I didn't know one way or the other."

Still, Rick agreed to take on the project as part of his Black Belt training, and formed a cross-functional team representing warehouse staff, engineering, and finance. Since no one knew how much inventory there was at first, let alone how much there *should* be, they set a goal that encompassed that uncertainty:

Reduce inventory to an optimum level

And of course determining just what the optimum level was became part of the project.

Team
Greg Meszaros, Champion; Michele Hill, Advisor; Roger Hirt, Advisor; Rick Orr, Project Leader/Black Belt; Dave Pepper, warehouse; Nate Parker, warehouse; Lori Dekoninck, warehouse; Phyllis Davis, engineering admin.; Steve Davis, Assistant Traffic Engineer; Tracy Neumeier, Internal Audit/Black Belt

---

The Investigation

The first question facing the team was "is this really a problem?" The warehouse had no formal system of inventory tracking. So being a finance guy, Rick looked to invoices and historical work orders to get a few interesting numbers (see Table C, next page).

Table C: Expenses, Usage, and Inventory	
Actual material expense 2001	$636,865
Actual material expense 2002	$584,287
Actual material expense 2003 thru 9/30	$320,199
total	**$1,541,351**
Historical usage captured	
Jan. '01 – Sept. '03, valued at	**$966,547**
Inventory value as of...	
Sept. 30, 2003	**$630,806**

If you don't have a calculator handy, we'll spare you the math: these numbers don't add up. There's more than $50,000 worth of inventory that isn't accounted for by purchases over the 34-month period. This mismatch is reflected in another way (see Figure 34).

Figure 34: Expenditures Don't Match Usage!

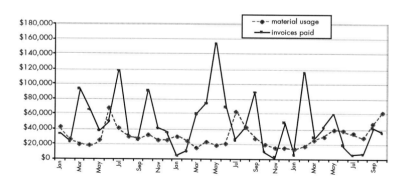

The key point of this chart is that the amount of money going out (invoices paid) is consistently higher than the amount of material actually used.

These figures did seem to validate that there was a problem that should be investigated. But at this point, the team had no idea why these figures didn't match. It could be that the records were incomplete. Or the department was building up inventory that wasn't being used. Which was it? The answer wouldn't come easily.

Rick was not alone

"When I started the accident reduction project in 2000, our records were just pitiful," says Christine Bowers, Assistant Chief of Fire Prevention. "I had a hard time finding data and information. We had boxes of records here and there, no rhyme or reason. There had not been an accident review board for several years, so the accidents were not getting reviewed. No discipline had been implemented, so we were sort of starting from scratch. In 1999, we thought there were16 accidents. It could be a lot higher than that. We just didn't have all the data. So you see that the numbers of accidents seem to be increasing at the start of the project, but it's because we were getting better records, not that there were more accidents."

Solutions & Results

"The initial problem was that we were starting from ground zero," says Rick. "We had no idea of what was on hand or how quickly it was being used up. The breakthrough moment for me was discovering that there was a Microsoft Access template for inventory control that we could use."

Phase 1: Establish the database

As Rick worked with the team to create the new inventory database, he discovered that there were some items that weren't—in the words of the warehouse guys—"on the books" (which meant listed in an Excel spreadsheet). That turned out to be about 4% of the warehouse items. So the first step was making sure that everything was listed in the database—and at least data on levels is now more accurate than it was at the start of the project.

Phase 2: Try to establish usage rates

Unlike the Excel spreadsheet, which was overwritten each month and therefore did not record previous inventory levels, the new Access system could tell you inventory levels for any given date. "That meant I could start tracking actual usage," says Rick. "But since I could only get  a data point per month, it was going to take a while to establish usage rates—or demand rate, really—with the new database."

Phase 3: Enter the Kanban system

About this time the city Master Black Belt ran across some old training materials he had on inventory control. He gave the materials to Rick, who learned about the Kanban (cahn-bahn) system for the first time.

Kanban is a modern inventory management practice invented at Toyota. The basic logic is simple:

- Inventory ties up money that you could be using elsewhere.

- You want to minimize the dollars invested while still enabling trouble-free operations.

- The optimal level depends on how quickly something is used up, adjusted by a risk factor: "You have to balance the risk of running out of something against the risk represented by having too much money tied up in inventory," explains Rick.

The way that Kanban works, Rick continues, is by establishing the maximum number of any item you should have on hand at any given point in time, and a minimum number that should trigger a reorder. "So you have an upper limit and a lower limit," Rick says. "You order when you reach the lower limit up to the upper limit. It's really simple once you get the right data to determine the maximum and minimum levels."

The Kanban formula is based on four factors:

1. **Demand** – the average monthly usage amount

2) **Lead time** – length of time between placing order and receiving goods, measured in monthly units

3) **Order interval** – how often orders are anticipated, in monthly units

4) **Safety stock** – amount of inventory to be held to compensate for variability in demand and/or lead time

The key factor here is safety stock, says Rick. "You make a decision—at the executive level—about how much risk you're willing to take that you'll run out of something. Generally the decision is based on how critical the service is that you're providing."

For example, most of the time the street light unit replaces a burned-out light bulb within 24 hours, but once in a while if they run out it might take longer. "The safety stock question is how critical it is that a street light is replaced immediately. Can we afford to wait an extra day in order to carry less inventory overall? The more risk you're willing to take, the less inventory."

Results

With the Kanban system up and running, street light inventory has dropped steadily since the project began in mid-2003 (see Figure 35, next page). This is turn has freed up budgetary resources (see Figure 36, next page).

Figure 35:
Steady Drop in Street Light Inventory

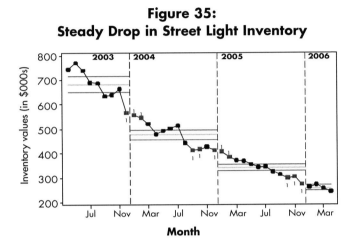

Through December 2005, $500,000 has been made available for use elsewhere. Without this project, inventory would likely be at the level it was in early 2003.

Figure 36:
Better Data Allows Lower Inventory Budgets

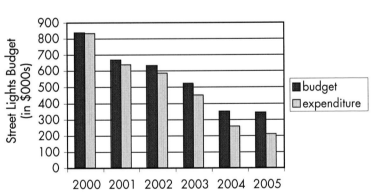

In May 2003, the inventory budget was reduced by $100,000 in anticipation of project success. In June 2004, the inventory budget was decreased an additional $150,000.

There is one thing that Rick finds troubling: "To date, we've never run out of anything," he says. "If you never run out, you're carrying too much inventory. I suspect that the level of safety stock is too high—and that we're still tying up too much money in inventory—money that could be put to better use elsewhere in the city. I'm eager to see if these figures are going to stabilize."

Rick Orr with a much-reduced stack of components used to build street lights.

What Made This Work

- **Setting up systems to collect data.** As Rick discovered, in many cases the data you need to make good decisions simply doesn't exist—or isn't easily accessible. Your teams will likely run into this same problem, so you'll need to tack on extra time at the beginning of a project simply to get the data collection systems up and running.

- **Using the data the system collects.** When you don't have data, you have to base decisions on intuition, experience, and gut feeling. And sometimes you'll make a good decision. But, especially in cases like this, a lot of times you won't. As Rick's project shows, there's a lot of potential for making better use of monetary resources when you have data to help you make decisions about appropriate inventory levels.

CHAPTER 6

A Revolution of Improvement

From 0 to 60 in nothing flat

As I quoted in Chapter 1, Roger Hirt, our Master Black Belt, always talks about how it took a **revolution, not an evolution,** in improvement capability to get us where we are today. He's right. We started from a place where people weren't sure they even had customers or processes. Now I hear many city employees ask one of my favorite questions: "Where's the data?"

Because of the general inexperience with improvement, we knew that we'd have to follow every project closely and provide a lot of coaching, education, and support. That dictated the need for three elements:

1. We really needed to select a few high-impact, high-visibility efforts. That meant shaping a very **targeted effort**.

2. We also knew that involvement in our Six Sigma projects would require extra effort by participants because they wouldn't be pulled out of their regular jobs. And *that* dictated that we use a **volunteer deployment model:** we needed to have people who were enthusiastic about being involved and, while not eager to work overtime, would be much more

willing to do so than someone who was being forced to participate.

3. If you're using a volunteer model, you need to create an environment where people want to get involved— to **create pull**, in other words.

In this chapter, we'll look at all three of these elements.

Element #1: Targeting

One of the commonly acknowledged shortcomings of the quality initiatives in the 1980s was that companies more or less let anyone work on any problem that interested them. While well-intentioned, that feel-good approach resulted in a lot of money and effort being spent on initiatives that made little difference in performance outcomes. And why would business leaders continue to support something that merely drained their coffers?

To create change that is more than a flash in the pan, you have to use Lean and Six Sigma on problems or issues that really matter. Or, as I often ask my division and department heads, **"What keeps you up at night?"** There were a lot of answers to that question, everything from constant customer complaints to a backlog of work, to a need to cut red tape, to concerns about being able to get everything done within budget allotments.

No matter what the answer, I'd talk with these people about how Six Sigma could help solve the problem. That alone planted the seed that Six Sigma wasn't something people felt they had to do but instead was something that could help them with the things that mattered most. The discussions also fed into deliberations about where to do our first Six Sigma projects, and suddenly we were making progress on strategic issues.

It was also important to choose projects that had a direct impact on our strategic goals of having a Safe City, gaining and retaining quality Jobs, and our B.E.S.T. (Building Excellent Service with Teams) initiative. Cutting red tape for new investments and filling potholes in 1.5 hours instead of 4 days were highly visible achievements that contributed to our strategic goals.

Element #2: Fort Wayne's Deployment Model

There are three elements in our Lean Six Sigma deployment that were identical to those you'd see in a successful business deployment:

- The effort was led by the top executive (the Mayor; comparable to a CEO in business)
- Lean Six Sigma was viewed as critical for achieving business priorities, not as a separate effort done just to improve
- We used the full repertoire of Lean Six Sigma improvement methods for studying problems, collecting and analyzing data, mapping processes, and so on

In all other respects, however, the challenges of deploying Lean Six Sigma in government meant we couldn't do things exactly the way they are done in the private sector. To understand why, let's first look at Lean Six Sigma deployment in business, then compare that to the realities of city government.

The most important elements

The first two bullets listed here—executive leadership and viewing Lean Six Sigma as a strategic priority—are often cited as the most important factors that determine whether Lean Six Sigma thrives in a business. With those factors present, questions about investing in Lean Six Sigma become practical, not theoretical. There will still be negotiation around how much the company can afford to do, but no arguments about whether it *should* be done. That level of commitment must be present no matter what the venue.

Lean Six Sigma in Business

Companies that have been most successful with Lean Six Sigma have made substantial investments in deployment by:

- Nominating a senior executive (often called a Champion) who is responsible for overall results of the deployment, and leads the planning and oversees execution. In the best companies, this is a full-time position that reports directly to the CEO.

- Training some percentage of the workforce in Lean Six Sigma methods. Trainees are "certified" at various skill levels depending on how much training they receive and the amount of project work they complete. The titles for the skill levels are styled after the martial arts:

- **Green Belts** are people who have completed a short introductory program, typically two days to one week, that provides a basic knowledge of Lean Six Sigma. In most companies, they also serve as project team members.

- **Black Belts** receive much more extensive training, usually four full weeks spread out over several months, and are required to *lead* an improvement project as part of the training. Once certified—training complete and project results verified—they serve as the primary resources within the organization for Lean Six Sigma projects. Some companies have trained 1% to 2% of their workforce at the Black Belt level.

- A small subset of Black Belts goes on to complete advanced training and more project work. These **Master Black Belts** serve as mentors for Black Belts, advise project teams, and coach sponsors.

• Deploying the Black Belts and Master Black Belts full-time to improvement work. (Not all companies make that level of commitment, but it is typical of the ones that have demonstrated sustainable success with Lean Six Sigma.)

• Placing Return on Investment (ROI) demands on each Black Belt. In larger companies, this can be as high as several hundred thousand dollars in increased revenues, savings, and/or cost avoidance that each Black Belt is expected to generate per year. In some companies, a portion of a Black Belt's pay is tied to their Lean Six Sigma results.

• Making Lean Six Sigma participation a *requirement* for advancement.

Most people working in city government will go down this list of typical Lean Six Sigma deployment requirements and say "We can't do that" to most if not all the items:

- The city's CEO (Mayor, City Manager) rarely has authority to create new full-time positions (equivalent to the Champion and Black Belts). We hope to get more buy-in for doing so in the future, but in the meantime we have had to ask our Belts to do their project work in addition to their regular responsibilities.

- Since city budgets usually need the approval of a city council, allocating significant funds for Lean Six Sigma work is usually a pipe dream at first (unless the council is leading the charge, which was not the case in Fort Wayne). We have worked out ways to get training at much lower costs than our private sector counterparts (see p. 181., but have encountered some project delays because of budgeting issues. See the sidebar (below) for one example.

- Though the city CEO can make Lean Six Sigma a requirement for advancement in some positions, being Mayor is like being the temporary CEO of a

"I started my Green Belt project in 2001, but it took over a year to complete. The long delay was because we had to buy a $35,000 phosphorus analyzer, and it wasn't in the budget for that year, so it took me a year to get it through the budget cycle."

Joe Johnson, Program Manager of Combined Sewer Overflow

"permanent" workforce (at least as permanent as jobs are these days). So people are less likely to feel that their jobs are at risk if they don't participate. Our tactic has been to make participation something that people *want* to do voluntarily for the contribution it makes to their work and also to their professional development (see p. 191).

- Public sector entities will be limited in their ability to tie financial rewards to an individual's Lean Six Sigma performance. However, some financial rewards can be tied to overall performance with contract workgroups. There was an example of this in the discussion of Bob Kennedy's project (see p. 39).

As this book proves, these hurdles did not derail our Lean Six Sigma efforts. Here's more detail on how we made it all work in Fort Wayne.

Lean Six Sigma in Fort Wayne

When a CEO like GE's Jack Welch tells his company that they are going to do Six Sigma—and that future promotions will be based in part on Six Sigma experience—you can be sure that participation is seen as a mandate. Most mayors would be hard pressed to wield that kind of power. I was no exception. So we used what I think of as a "leaders and volunteers" deployment model instead of a "CEO mandate." It was very important that:

1. We bring people together both within and across departments, and even from outside the organization
2. We find a way to offer Cadillac training at a Cavalier price
3. We provide overall guidance for the initiative

Deployment Theme #1: Bringing people together

As you can tell from the featured projects, the majority of our improvement efforts have involved teams of people coming together to solve problems. This did NOT occur because we announced "we're all going to work in teams now." I've seen eyes roll when you try to build teamwork that way. Rather, we created the expectation that anyone who was working on improvement would involve others who had relevant knowledge, which usually meant other people in the work area, customers, and/or suppliers.

This approach to teamwork fed into several objectives:

- First, research shows that creativity is often greater when people work in teams than when they work alone (as long as all team members get a chance to contribute). So we expected better solutions through teamwork.

- Team participation was a good way to expose people to the methods/tools prior to any official training. Being part of a group where most members were new to this stuff helped make everyone more comfortable with learning. Also, people involved on teams became witnesses who could provide firsthand testimony to the usefulness of the tools/methods.

- In many cases, the "people with relevant knowledge" were *outside* the department where the improvement was occurring. Thus by default we created cross-functional communication, which later spilled over into other work—people from different departments who have worked together on a project are more likely to call each other when other issues arise.

Because teamwork was an embedded expectation of the process, we avoided the dysfunction that sometimes occurs with forced teamwork and all the meaningless talk that has to accompany such an effort. If you could drop by a team meeting it's unlikely you'd hear team members complain about having to be there. They don't see their attendance as a waste of time because they know they have knowledge or expertise that's useful to the project, and that if they are successful, their jobs will be easier or more rewarding in some way.

Deployment Theme #2: Cadillac training at a Cavalier price

Would you want a brain surgeon who had only half the training? Perhaps the comparison is extreme, but the point is the same: you can't expect your Lean or Six Sigma projects to be successful if the people leading them aren't fully trained. However, training is costly. It's not unusual for businesses to spend anywhere from $20,000 to $50,000 training a single Black Belt or Master Black Belt—which doesn't seem that high when you consider that these people are expected to generate ten times as much in savings or revenue *per year*.

Obviously, there was no way we were able to make that kind of investment. Our solution? We were able to partner with the local TQM Network to get the same training that private sector employees receive, at a fraction of the usual cost. (A local division of ITT also trained two of our Black Belts as a cooperative gesture to the city.) Our city employees attend the same sessions as people from the private sector, a cross-fertilization that has proved useful:

> *"My Black Belt class included people from a local manufacturer. Their jobs were on the line. Their whole company was about to go under. I was surprised by the intensity of their Six Sigma projects—this wasn't about whether or not they could get a little better, this was about whether or not they survived. The exposure to people from other sectors made me appreciate the opportunity I had to be there and get that caliber of training. Also, we had this pride thing going on—we wanted to show that city people could do as well as the private sector people! That was a real driver."*
>
> Greg Meszaros
> Director of City Utilities and Public Works

The training provided by the TQM Network is a typical Black Belt course, four full weeks of training (160 hours) covering topics ranging from process thinking to data collection, problem solving, and multiple data analysis tools. The training is in four week-long sessions one month apart. Between training weeks, participants work on their projects, applying what they've just learned. (Adding to challenge for our employees is that this project work is on top of their other responsibilities; many of their private sector counterparts get to work full-time (or nearly so) on their projects.

Our first Black Belt was Michele Hill, who was acting as our Quality Manager at the time (more about her in a little bit). She started the training in February 2000. Since then we have sent more than 30 people through the training in groups of two to six. Twelve are officially certified as Black Belts, meaning they have completed at least one project, have demonstrated the ability to use and understand the Six Sigma statistical tools, and have the support of our Master Black Belt and their manager/sponsor. Many others are still working to complete their projects or are in training; a handful have moved on to jobs outside the city, and a few had projects that were abandoned for various reasons.

Michele Hill, our first Black Belt and Quality Manager

As Mayor, one of the things I learned in my previous careers was that great communication and people skills are often more important than subject matter expertise when it comes to implementing change. So when I was looking for someone to coordinate the initial Six Sigma efforts within Fort Wayne, I picked Michele Hill even though she had no prior experience with Six Sigma itself. She was then the assistant to my chief of staff, had a broad background in corporate training and program development, and was widely known as someone who was really great at dealing with people. Her accomplishments have since let her move into a similar position in the healthcare field, which was one of her career goals. See the next two pages for details.

"I have a good friend from college who earned a degree in engineering then went to work for GE. She and I met for dinner about a year after she took the job and she kept talking about this thing called "Black Belt" training that she was getting involved in. I remember  thinking at the time 'why is GE wasting such an intelligent and talented person on Six Sigma?' In the years of earning my degree in political science, I had not been exposed to any quality methods or tools in my course work. Six Sigma was a completely foreign and misunderstood concept to me.

"That's why I find it ironic that just a few years later I was asked by the Mayor to take Black Belt training myself and become the Quality Manager for Fort Wayne. Frankly, I thought I wasn't the right person. I will admit to being a statistics-phobe before this program.

"In February 2000 I became the first city employee to go through the training. And the more I got into my project, the more I saw how statistics had a practical use. I became comfortable with Six Sigma pretty quickly. I really liked the step-by-step problem solving, the team focus, and how it helped people do their jobs better.

"My job during those first years was to help put the structures in place for getting the training and projects done, to mentor the trainees, coordinate projects, and work with managers and supervisors all across the city to make sure they were comfortable with what was going on. I wasn't a Master Black Belt who could provide a lot of technical advice to people, but I did meet with the Black Belts regularly to make sure they were following the methodology. And I attended project team meetings if they needed help.

"I was glad I caught onto the methodology quickly, but it did turn out that my people skills were my most important asset. I had to be able to interact with people who were leery of what was going on. I had to help convince them that Six Sigma wasn't a scary thing, that we weren't there to take anybody's job away or point fingers. We wanted to work together to help them get rid of problems and improve the way the city operated.

"We did a lot of things right. We picked some very good people and very good projects. I had the opportunity to work with a lot of wonderful people. It was exciting to think that Fort Wayne was really a pioneer in this field.

"My advice to other cities is to get the broader leadership engaged earlier in their efforts that we did, to make it mandatory for division and department heads to become familiar with Six Sigma. I think we could have communicated better with the City Council to gain their support earlier on, too.

"I'm very grateful for my experience with the City of Fort Wayne. I think Six Sigma has brought something amazing both to me personally and to Fort Wayne. It's great that we are role models for the rest of the country.

—Michele Hill, the first Fort Wayne Black Belt

How our training works

Originally, we thought we'd be able to train more Black Belts more quickly, but when it became clear that we were strained to the edges of our capacity (in terms of time and expenses), and that there was political opposition to doing more, we realized we needed to attack our training goals in smaller chunks.

So a year later, in May 2001, we developed and launched our Green Belt training, which we deliver internally using our Black Belts. This course is a total of 80 hours, done in sessions of one full day (8 hours) per week for 10 consecutive weeks. (We know other organizations do Green Belt training in two 40-hour weeks, but taking people away from their jobs for that much time all at once wasn't feasible in our environment.) The training is nearly as broad as that for Black Belts, but not nearly as deep. The Black Belts get a few more advanced tools and go into more detail about the why and how of each tool; Green Belt training is mostly an introduction so that people will recognize concepts and tools, but aren't expected to apply them without guidance and support.

Deployment Theme #3: Good oversight of the initiative

In a business, the Champion and executive leadership team usually lead the strategic oversight of Lean and Six Sigma efforts. For us, the equivalent was creating a Quality Council, comprising me, Michele Hill, and several other people. The council was very helpful initially in creating shared ownership and in providing a venue for sharing ideas about what should be attempted.

However, I have to admit that the original council eventually drifted apart. It met only sporadically and was treated as its own silo (that is, not well linked to core functions or even to the rest of the Six Sigma effort)—and therefore its usefulness and influence was limited. What we learned was that we needed to make it the focal point for linking Six Sigma and Lean to the organization.

"The first time I heard about Six Sigma was from the Mayor in 1999. But then there was a group that went through the first training wave, and I started hearing more about it from them in 2000.

"What's nice about [our Six Sigma program] is that you're studying processes in the areas you work on every day ... so you're comfortable with what you're doing, the statistics you're analyzing.

"Secondly, the software packet that we used made the statistical analysis much easier than I thought it would be.

"Finally, the classes themselves were great. It's one week out of the month for four months in a row, and that made it easier."

—Phil GiaQuinta

So we resurrected it as the Learning and Quality Enhancement Council in May 2005. The new council has nine members, including city staff and two outside advisers:

- **The Mayor (me) and the Deputy Mayor:** The deputy mayor and I represent the strategic vision and provide the organizational authority to make things happen.

- **The City Controller:** When done correctly, Six Sigma and Lean efforts have significant impact on the city budget, both in terms of resources consumed and the savings generated. Having fiscal responsibility represented on the Council is therefore essential for proper management of the initiatives and the city as a whole.

- **Three Directors** (public information, human resources, and public works and utilities): Why these particular three?
  - I suspect every city in the same situation would choose the first two: Public Information because the ability to implement Six Sigma and Lean is largely dependent on the support you are able to generate. Word-of-mouth helped within the city, but documenting our successes and gains, and making those facts known to the public, is key to getting support from both the public and our city council. Human Resources needs to be represented because of the impact on hiring, training, and resource usage.
  - Having a third or even fourth director will vary from city to city depending on circumstances. In our case, it turned out that our Public Works and City Utilities division was our "early adopter," generating successes

and getting lots of people involved early on. Its current director, Greg Meszaros, has been quoted many times in this book. Originally the Associate Director of City Utilities, he took the Black Belt training, led the water main project (p. 213), and was later promoted to the director position. So he is experienced in both doing Six Sigma and providing the leadership to expand its use within city government.

- **Our Professional Development and Diversity Manager:** In Chapter 4, I talked about the necessity of building leadership skills at all levels of the organization. That and the fact that Six Sigma affords many professional development opportunities to staff made it clear to us that we needed this manager on the Council.

- Our **Master Black Belt** and our **Quality Manager:** Currently, we have only one Master Black Belt for the city as a whole (that's Roger Hirt, who's been referenced several times in this book). He and our Quality Manager know the most about Six Sigma as a discipline and the practical aspects of implementation.

- The **president of the TQM Network** and **their TQM Master Black Belt.** These are our partners in implementation, not only providing critical guidance based on their extensive experience with Six Sigma but also linking us to resources we can draw on for training and education opportunities.

We have also defined more clearly the roles and responsibilities of the council, as shown in Table D (next page).

Table D:
Executive Quality Council Responsibilities

The Mayor's Executive Quality Council is responsible to the Mayor to plan, organize, and implement the City's quality initiatives. These initiatives include Six Sigma, B.E.S.T., Action Workout, and activity-based management.

Specific responsibilities of the Council are to:

1. Translate the Mayor's key goals into tangible and measurable metrics.
2. Identify focus areas that will assist in achieving the Mayor's key goals and metrics.
3. Develop a City "Quality Plan."
4. Charter significant and realistic projects.
5. Identify the appropriate quality methodology to accomplish the project.
6. Select City employees to receive training and lead projects.
7. Create a project database.
8. Manage deployment using consistent and meaningful metrics.
9. Recommend reward and recognition opportunities for successful teams.
10. Assure that internal and external mechanisms are in place to measure and validate the value of projects.
11. Communicate the City's quality initiatives and successes to City employees and to the public.

The responsibilities of the original council were less results-oriented—one of the oversights that automatically made it peripheral in importance. As you can see, the new council is not only responsible for defining metrics (item #8) but also for validating project outcomes (item #10). Those two responsibilities automatically put the council in the position of having to police its own effectiveness as well as that of the entire Six Sigma initiative because it raises critical questions: Are we looking at the right metrics? How would we know? Are we getting the results we want? How do we know? What do we have to change to better track performance and to get better results?

I've come to believe that getting an effective Quality Council (or something like it) up and running early in the deployment is one way to drive adoption of Lean and Six Sigma much more quickly. I would urge all mayors considering this path to make sure their Quality Councils really hum.

Element #3: Creating Pull for Lean Six Sigma

To date the vast majority of our Lean and Six Sigma efforts have been done by volunteers (the only mandate in the deployment was that department heads attend the two-day Champion training). That was a strategic choice. Recall that I had won my first election with the slimmest of margins. There was a highly charged political environment in the sense that I was not the candidate endorsed by many of the unions. I was not a person that everybody knew; I was an unknown in city government. So there was a lot of uncertainty around who would keep their jobs, who wouldn't; here's a Democrat coming in where a Republican had been for more than a decade; how's he going to work with a still Republican-controlled city council.

In short, I knew that Six Sigma and Lean would have to sell themselves as much as possible. So I had to rely on what you might call the **contagion of success** deployment model, or what my manufacturing friends would call a **pull system:** getting to the point where people *ask* to get involved because they see the benefits to themselves personally and to their work areas. A number of factors discussed already in this book fed into creating pull:

- Having volunteers working on projects of personal interest to them meant there was a level of enthusiasm that might not have been present if participation had been mandatory or if projects had been chosen for them. The Black Belt and Green Belt trainees were really motivated to succeed.

- The projects had to be important to the departments, meaning the results would contribute to strategic goals by making a noticeable impact on customers, budgets, and/or performance targets. That requirement increased the level of support the team could expect from its manager/sponsor, coworkers, and even customers and suppliers.

- Success with these projects spoke more loudly than any words I could say to people. Non-participants began to believe that Six Sigma or Lean was something they should get involved in; team members wanted to build on what they'd already learned; Black Belts wanted to tackle bigger projects.

- Citizens, customers, and people from other departments who were involved in the projects began spreading the word.

We also did a lot of work on three other fronts:

1. Overcoming resistance through involvement.

2) Emphasizing ways in which people could personally benefit from involvement. The options ranged from getting a feeling of accomplishment to earning financial incentives in some cases and opening more opportunities for promotion.

3) Creating a culture of local heroes: publicizing and celebrating participants' achievements and successes.

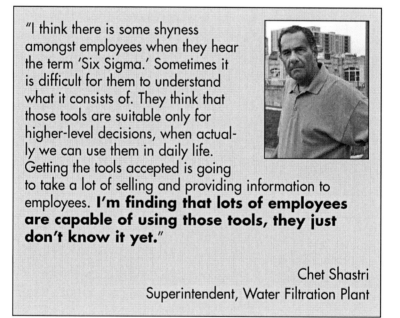

"I think there is some shyness amongst employees when they hear the term 'Six Sigma.' Sometimes it is difficult for them to understand what it consists of. They think that those tools are suitable only for higher-level decisions, when actually we can use them in daily life. Getting the tools accepted is going to take a lot of selling and providing information to employees. **I'm finding that lots of employees are capable of using those tools, they just don't know it yet.**"

Chet Shastri
Superintendent, Water Filtration Plant

1. Overcoming Resistance Through Involvement

I'll let our City Utilities Services Manager, Phil GiaQuinta, explain this point for me. "The hardest part—and I don't think this is true for just government—is that people are resistant to change," says Phil. "I've had some people decline to get involved. But I found that, in general, if you can talk to people and put them on your team or committee, and make them inclusive in the change and decision making, you're much better off."

Phil adds that having Lean and Six Sigma methods are critical elements as well. "In a sense, by going through the process [of data gathering and problem analysis], you're proving it to your committee. You're telling them, 'Here's our problem and if we do these changes, life will be better for all of us.' As a result, it's not like *imposing* change on people, it's them deciding that doing the work differently is the best decision."

Resistance to change is part of the Lean Six Sigma package, and it's important that you understand where that resistance is coming from. Here are three examples:

- "Some staff here were reluctant at first," says Utility Services Manager Gina Kostoff. "They just weren't comfortable with the new, unfamiliar tools. But I was coming in as a new manager and took the time to look at the things we do. The first few days of Lean training, people were honest and said they didn't want to be there. But now that they've seen how it can make their jobs easier, they embrace it. Now I have people coming to me and asking the critical question: '*Why* are we doing that?' As a result, we've found that in many instances, there simply *was* no reason for performing some tasks other than we always did it that way or it used to be a requirement."

- Paul Spoelhof of our Community Development Department says the kind of resistance he encounters is a bit different. "It's not a resistance of 'I don't want to do this,'" says Paul. "It's a resistance that stems from 'how do we do this and get all our other stuff done, too?' It's been frustrating at times, but eventually we were able to take small chunks of our long-range plan and implement those pieces." Paul also points to the more inclusive approach his department is using as part of the solution to external resistance. "We're taking the position that our role in city government is to provide leaders and create the vision," he says. "We engage other interests from around the city—the community, homebuilders, non-profit health chains, foundations, private entrepreneurs—in helping to shape that vision so everyone can get into it."

Paul adds that he's since learned there's a name for this phenomenon. "We were reading Peter Senge's book and I saw that what I'd seen happening was called creating a shared vision."

It was an aha moment for him. "That leadership role, getting involved with agencies as a partner, is something relatively new," he says. "People tell me that they feel there is more true involvement on every side, and not that the city is being dictatorial. They appreciate that."

- Matthew Wirtz was part of the engineering team that has saved the city thousands and thousands of dollars through the water main project you can read about on p. 213. "The biggest resistance we encountered was from the maintenance department staff, which wasn't too surprising," he recalls. "They'd been using and trusting a certain type of pipe material for a long, long time. And they have the right to be opinionated, since they have to deal with water mains long after the engineering role is done." Once again the answer was education and involvement.

Leadership support also key to working through resistance

Broad involvement is just one strategy we used to reduce or at least work through resistance. Another key element is visible support by the organization's leaders. Maria Gomez-Espino, a program manager in City Utilities, is also the Lean champion. Having shepherded more than 32 Lean projects to completion, she takes the message of visible leadership support to heart. In her own words:

"Realistically, we expect resistance to Lean just as there is to Six Sigma. People are naturally concerned about what it means, and whether there's a threat that they'll lose their jobs," she says. *"There's value in educating people ahead of time, talking to them about what's really involved, what the goals and purpose are, and helping them understand what's in it for them."* Maria uses this same approach when launching a new project. *"I sit down with the manager and their process expert or even an entire work group prior to a Kaizen event, and work with the individuals to scope out the project and figure out what we would like to accomplish."* At the same time, she adds, she's educating them about what Lean involves and their role in supporting the efforts.

2. Perks of Personal Involvement ("What's In It For Me")

Like many service organizations, 80% of the city's budget is in payroll. If I had come in saying that Six Sigma was a way to cut $10 million from the budget, people would have immediately translated that into "I'm going to lose my job." Losing jobs was the furthest thing from my mind.

So the first step in creating support for Six Sigma is to avoid positioning the effort as something that can harm employees' jobs. The second step is the flipside: emphasizing all the ways in which involvement in Six Sigma can benefit people individually ("What's in it for me?" or WIIFM):

- They're going to reduce the time it takes to do time-consuming things, therefore giving themselves more time to do the things they like to do and that are beneficial

- They're going to delight customers through improved processes and faster cycle time

- They'll understand their jobs better and be in a position of greater decision-making responsibility

- They'll have greater pride of ownership

- They're going to gain a marketable skill set (demand for Six Sigma skills is so great that certified Green or Black Belts often command a 15-20% premium in the job market)

Position "losses" from Six Sigma gains

I can't say we haven't lost any employees as a result of our performance enhancement programs. It's fair to say that we haven't had any employees *laid off* because of our efforts.

However, our combined Public Works and City Utilities division has used Lean and Six Sigma, among other tools, to aggressively manage attrition. Their staffing levels are down 8% even though their systems and the population served by their services is growing.

How did they do this? For one thing, the division plans Lean and Six Sigma projects in areas where it has upcoming retirements to prepare the organization to update the work practices before the employees retire. Also, there is no shortage of work to do, so any gains in time are used to handle more of the existing workload. Thirdly, each time an employee retires or leaves for another position they always ask "do we have to fill this position?"

In truth, we *have* lost several city employees as a result of Six Sigma—because of job opportunities that opened up to them in the private sector. For example, Michele Hill, our first Black Belt and citywide champion for several years, out-competed a number of other candidates for a Six Sigma leadership job in the private sector, as described on pp. 184–185.

The WIIFM can be even more explicit if you tie Six Sigma or Lean participation and results to either financial incentives or promotion opportunities, as discussed below.

Financial incentives

In many private companies, part of a Black Belt's compensation is tied to the results of their Six Sigma projects. In the public sector, it's difficult to work on the basis of individual rewards for individual effort, but we've been working to weave performance-based goals and compensation into contracts. Currently, 7 of our 11 union collective bargaining contracts have provisions related to divisions or departments meeting goals that are then quantified, measured, and rewarded with real money from a pot.

One example of that was Bob Kennedy's pothole repair project (see table on p. 39). Our collective bargaining contracts through the water filtration plant also contain incentives that financially reward all employees for meeting various department-wide cost-structure goals for operating the water plant. We like these financial incentives because they allow rank-and-file employees to share in the success of our performance enhancement programs.

The incentives are not directly tied to Six Sigma or Lean projects as you might find in the private sector. But simply having performance goals does encourage people to be interested in ways to improve how their jobs are done.

Promotion expectations

The logic here is simple: if you think that Lean Six Sigma is one of the best ways to become a world-class business, then you want people with Lean Six Sigma experience running the organization. People who have training and project experience will be more attuned to customer needs; they'll see how work processes impact each other; they'll routinely use data in decision making without being prompted. And they'll be better able to evaluate potential investments in Lean Six Sigma projects.

The strategy has worked well in leading companies, where managers (or managerial candidates) spend perhaps two years as Black Belts then rotate into the next higher level of management.

We've had a number of Six Sigma and Lean participants who have received promotions in whole or in part because of those experiences. Performance evaluations for all division heads and many department heads use Six Sigma as a specific criteria.

3. Creating Local Heroes by Celebrating Successes

Politically minded readers probably need no explanation about why we take every opportunity to advertise and celebrate our Lean Six Sigma and other successes. For one thing, we are more limited than our private sector counterparts in how we can express appreciation for these efforts. So making local heroes of our Black Belts, Green Belts, and other team participants is a great way to demonstrate to them and to everyone watching that their work is valued and appreciated.

Some specific steps we've taken include:

- I personally attend all ceremonies where a Black Belt or Green Belt is certified (which happens when the results of their projects are verified). I also try to drop in on every Black Belt and Green Belt training program at least once.
- We have a Black Belt or Green Belt share their story as a standard agenda item in the meetings I have with all department heads.
- We always feature a Green Belt or Black Belt project in the city newsletter that goes to all employees.

Six Sigma Showcase

To help build credibility for our investments in Six Sigma and Lean, we started holding community-wide celebrations once a year, called Six Sigma Showcases. These celebrations are typically luncheon meetings featuring a guest speaker like Michael George, Wayne Iurillo (Raytheon's Site Executive), or Lou Dollive (ITT Aerospace Division CEO). Black Belts from both city and private sector projects are invited to share storyboard presentations, which line the perimeter of the luncheon room. Several hundred people came to our last such event. What's great is that Fort Wayne city projects get featured right alongside projects from local companies.

Lean Six Sigma Showcase, September 2006

The showcase events we put together have proven to be a fun way to recognize the contributions of those who have led or supported projects.

Attendees include city staff and private sector business people interested in promoting operational excellence in city government.

Project leaders display summaries of their team's work, and get a chance to discuss what they learned and accomplished with me, their coworkers, and quality professionals.

The public meetings serve several purposes. For one thing, if you're out there talking about saving $1.7 million, it's very hard for criticism to mount. For another, it's simply good business to demonstrate to your customers (all of whom are also taxpayers) how the city is working to provide better services while holding down costs.

Lessons Learned #5

Several lessons emerged right away in the first years of our deployments:

1. We might have moved faster had we had training tailored to government employees

As discussed above, we piggybacked our Black Belt training on courses already being taught locally—which, as it happened, were developed for people in the manufacturing sector. This added a level of challenge for people who were being exposed to quality improvement for the first time: many of the concepts and tools are hard enough to understand the first time through without having them couched in manufacturing terms that mean little to you!

It would have been easier for our trainees if there had been more examples and applications shown for services or government. Getting examples from government (especially ones that don't come from Fort Wayne!) is still a challenge, but there are many, many service companies and service/administration functions of manufacturing companies that have used Lean Six Sigma, so finding examples that are more relevant to government employees is possible.

2. The strategic oversight is critical

Though we established a Quality Council early on, in hindsight I think we should have paid more attention to the importance of its role. It did serve a limited but valuable purpose in the early going, mostly as a kind of support group for the core team trying to make Six Sigma a reality in city government. But it could have played an even stronger role in driving Six Sigma and Lean had we constructed it then like we have it constructed today.

3. Deployment is easier in some departments than in others

If you've read this whole book, you know that we have a lot of examples from people in the various public works departments (such as streets, water, sewers) and a few more administrative function (such as finance). Deployment of Six Sigma and Lean has taken off in those departments, in part because we have a strong support from the division heads, but also, I believe, because the applications of the tools are easier to see in work areas that have data and easily visible processes.

In contrast, we're still working to find a model of deployment that works in areas like public safety. We've had sporadic, limited successes in police and fire in particular, but nothing that has really caught hold yet. Our plan is to focus more on the process and flow-oriented Lean tools that don't require the kind of data collection and analysis that is demanded by the Six Sigma methodologies. If you come up with models that work for you, please let us know.

Improving Our Improvements: the B.E.S.T. formal review

As I've tried to indicate with the "lessons learned" comments in each chapter, our deployment efforts were constantly being improved as we learned more about what worked for us and what didn't. As it happens, in July 2006 we completed a structured deployment-wide review, which was conducted by a team of 12 people—6 quality professionals from some of the largest businesses in our community and 6 city employees were involved in the deployment. The review included both online surveys and in-person interviews (the latter were done by the outsiders, with complete assurances of confidentiality).

Here are a few changes we've initiated as a result of this review:

1. Doing more to integrate the various methodologies in use

As described earlier in this chapter, we launched our improvement efforts primarily in the form of Six Sigma training and projects. A few years later, we implemented Lean-driven projects (based on the Kaizen model) and

Action Work Outs (a quick improvement methodology that works for narrowly focused problems). Treating all of these approaches as separate efforts has caused confusion and created a mindset that problems are *either* Lean or Six Sigma related. It has also led to misconceptions that Six Sigma projects are always long and complicated and that Lean tools can only be used in the context of the Kaizen events. Neither of those perceptions is true.

This confusion has caused us to reframe our language to emphasize the primary goal: **to create high-performance government in Fort Wayne**—and we'll use any and all tools and methods that will help us get there. We are also taking steps to always present Lean and Six Sigma as two sides of the same coin, and never present them as either/or. Rather, our mentality now is to use the appropriate tool for each situation.

2. Doing more to get our division and department leaders involved and committed

For the first five-plus years of deployment, the only *required* training was that division leaders complete the Executive Leadership two-day session. While having a basic understanding of Six Sigma is essential for leaders, we've learned that isn't enough—employees can interpret that as mere acceptance or compliance. Before we can expect employees to more fully commit themselves and their careers to continuous improvement, city leadership has to demonstrate its commitment.

To that end, we're taking steps to get division and department leaders more actively involved in the efforts. The task is a little easier now than in early years because we have solid results to show that Lean and Six Sigma are tools that can help them get more from their budgeted dollars. I also involved the division heads in a formal discussion of this very deployment report.

Each division head plus myself and the deputy mayor will now lead what we're calling Fast Action Lean Six Sigma projects. These projects combine the speed of our Lean projects with the data-driven analysis of the Six Sigma approach. In addition, project selection and championing will become a more critical part of executive leadership performance reviews.

3. Improving communication with all employees

The review team heard that many employees did not know what was happening with Six Sigma and Lean deployment in the city, or were unaware of the status of projects in their own work areas. This is a critical lapse because Six Sigma and Lean can be largely self-selling once employees experience the benefits firsthand and start talking to their peers about what they've gained by participation. A department-by-department rollout of project results and a communication plan is being developed.

4. Getting more out of our investment in Black Belts and Green Belts

Getting people trained as Black Belts and Green Belts is a struggle in a city government. Since we don't have the authority to create separate job positions, the people who volunteered for these positions had to somehow carve out time (and put in lots of extra hours) to complete their training and projects. During the review process, it became clear that we are developing a tremendous pool of talent and experience—which often goes underutilized after the projects are complete.

To get more out of this investment, we're working to create several full-time Black Belt positions so that those people can serve as resources to anyone in city government. That would give these people an opportunity to continue developing their skills and to help accelerate improvement efforts in the city. They would also then be available to help coach division and department leaders.

5. Formalizing our project selection process

In the early stages of many Lean Six Sigma deployments, the organizations let individual departments and work areas select their own projects because that's where they will have the passion needed to complete the work despite obstacles they encounter. As this book demonstrates, we haven't done too badly with that approach so far, but it's time to take it to the next level. There is now a process of formalizing our project selection approach, which includes more involvement by division and department leaders (see item #1 above) in discussions about where project investments will most benefit their work areas and its customers.

What We Need to Expand

In addition to learning about things we need to stop or start doing, the B.E.S.T. review exposed some areas where we've made a good start but could do more.

1. **Developing relationships with the union leadership:** Just as adopting Lean and Six Sigma has been patchy to some extent, so has our work to get the union leaders involved in championing the efforts as a way to improve the work skills of their members.

2. **Involving the finance area:** Knowing exactly what you're getting for your investment is a key tenet of Six Sigma—because it's that data that helps you get the most results for every dollar you put in. As the data charts spread throughout this book show, we're doing a good job of tracking the financial impact of some of our biggest projects. But one outcome of the review was that we need to do more to involve finance in helping to evaluate the potential impact of proposed projects and in validating project results across the board afterwards.

3. **Increasing the rewards and recognition for involvement and results:** This element has three distinct benefits:

   - First, in the public sector, we are limited in what we can do in terms of cash awards, raises, and promotions for people who get involved in our improvement efforts. The reputation that comes with having a successful project can in part compensate for our limitations with other kinds of rewards, and we need to do more to exploit that benefit.

- Second, as time goes by, we have to become more and more focused on *results* not just involvement. While having someone participate in a project is a great thing, the most important outcome is the improvement that will result in service to our community.

- Third, as just discussed above, we found that too many city employees didn't know what was happening in terms of improvement efforts. Doing more to publicize the results from their peers across the city will be part of our increased communication effort—and should generate increased interest from employees to get involved themselves.

> Perhaps the most profound impact of our Contagion of Success is that a lot of city employees are now convinced that **improvement is possible**. They *are* allowed to use their brains on the job—and all of them do. They start looking for better ways to do their work, outside the official Six Sigma framework.

Conclusion

The result, as you've seen throughout the book, has been overwhelmingly successful. There is now a deep commitment in our city government to continuous improvement. There are things we could have done differently or better (see the "Lessons Learned" at the end of many chapters), but we have built a lot of momentum very quickly, and produced some very impressive results.

This approach worked in part because our volunteers have become "learning leaders," people willing to take risks, face a challenge, take the initiative to solve problems. Having a core of these people out there being able to speak firsthand about their experiences offers much more powerful persuasion than anything I can do as Mayor. In fact, I've been told point-blank that if I had tried to mandate Six Sigma, I would have panicked a lot of people inside and outside the government, and would have ended up only creating a lot more resistance than anyone could hope to overcome.

A $300,000
Low-Hanging Fruit

in Water Main Replacement

I knew when launching Six Sigma that we'd find a lot of opportunities for making quick gains. I'd seen it happen every time an organization began to take improvement seriously. But the size of some of the low-hanging fruit in the city impressed even me. In this case, we had a performance goal that under conditions at that time would have cost $300,000 more than we could afford to spend. This became a low-hanging fruit because it took only a few very simple changes in policy— discovered by getting people in a room together—to bring the costs in line with our budget.

"In hindsight," says Greg Meszaros, "a lot of things that came out of this project seem simple. But they only popped out because we look at it in a structured way and used data to verify what our experts thought was happening."

Background

Fort Wayne is an old city by American standards. There is a network of 1,000 miles of water mains, much of which dates back to the late 1800s and early 1900s—meaning they are well over a century old! Most manufacturers recommend that water mains be replaced every 50 years.

"Even if you double that figure," comments project leader
Greg Meszaros, "and are willing to wait 100 years, the city
should be replacing a few
miles every year or you're
going to end up with a catas-

trophe." Ask residents of some older neighborhoods in Fort
Wayne and they'll tell you that day had already come and
gone. "In some neighborhoods, we'd get a water main break
three or four times a year," Greg says.

"Yet when Mayor Richard first took office, the city had
inadequately invested in water main replacement for many
years. That's unacceptable," says Greg. "Among other
things, it's a real public safety problem. That's why Mayor
Richard demanded that the utilities department start a
water main replacement program."

So in 2001, the department set a goal of replacing six miles
of water main per year. To get the work done, they followed
standard procedures: designing the project and putting it
out for bid. "We knew that to sustain the goal of six miles
of replacement we would need to reduce our cost structure,"
Greg explains. "Our bids were averaging $60 a foot or high-
er. That was more than we could afford if we were to meet
our goal of replacing six miles of water main per year."

Greg and his department didn't like the options at that
point. "We thought we'd either have to eat the cost or not
do the water main work—but then that would make the
problem worse," he says. "That's when the opportunity

came up for me to attend the Black Belt training, and I said I'll try using Six Sigma."

The Investigation

The progress from investigation to results doesn't come much faster than you'll find with this project.

"We put together a comprehensive team of everyone who works on this issue," says Greg. That included the engineers that design it, a construction manager, people who operate the water main once it's done, and contractors who bid on it. "Six Sigma really stresses the importance of taking a holistic view of a process," he adds. "So this was the first time we'd brought in an outside contractor to understand what it is they pay attention to when they bid for a project—what drives their costs."

Team
Ted Rhinehart, Champion; Greg Meszaros, Black Belt; Matthew Wirtz, Engineering; Mark Gensic, Engineering; Paul Powers, Engineering; Dan Smith, Construction Mgmt.; Ken Stempien,Construction Mgmt.; Bob Hinga, Maintenance; Outside advisors (contractors, private engineering firm)

What the team heard from the outside contractor opened a lot of eyes around the table. "We compared what our internal experts thought was important and what the contractor said was important," Greg says. "And the two were often the exact opposite."

Lesson 1: Fort Wayne's specs were antiquated

"The contractor told us that we were bidding jobs with materials and technology that were really antiquated," says Greg. "He said we were much too conservative in the spec we had." The specific problems? The city still primarily asked for bids involving the traditional ductile iron water mains, installed by open-trench digging. "The contractor said that the work he does in other cities is trenchless technology, using bored plastic pipe.

"So one of the first process hardening things we did is always give the contractor the choice of method and technology, traditional open cut or the bored plastic pipe. We will award on the lowest of those. That *immediately* lowered the cost structure of the bids. Contractors could now begin to bid using modern technology."

Here's a combination of old and new techniques not possible until this project: open-trench digging using plastic pipe material instead of traditional ductile iron.

Looking to Data for More Lessons

Like the sludge team described earlier, this group didn't stop once they had made some immediate gains. The fact that their assumptions had proved wrong in that case made the team eager to look for other assumptions they could test. So they decided they would look to data to see if their internal expert opinions were wrong in other ways.

Lesson #2: We were thinking too small

"Our engineers were convinced that we would get the most competitive bidding if we limited projects to about 5,000 feet at a time," says Greg. "And if we wanted to replace mains on three separate streets in a neighborhood, we'd bid them as three separate projects."

But when the team looked back at previous bids and talked to the contractors, they discovered this thinking was completely backwards. They learned that if the department bid really big footages—10,000 or 15,000 feet at time—that they would not only get better prices from the usual bidders but also attract more bidders to the process. As Greg points out, "There are a lot of contractors who won't bid a 3,000-foot job, but who will bid a 15,000-foot job."

The result? "Now, instead of doing six to eight smaller projects a year, we do two or three bigger ones," says Greg. "And if we have a lot of work in a neighborhood, we bid it all as one project."

Lesson #3: We needed to ask for bids in the winter months

"We used to ask for bids all year 'round," says Greg. But again, the team looked at the data and realized that they got much better prices on projects that were bid in the winter. "That's when the contractor is setting up for the year and can put in his best bid. Then when the weather gets nice, he knows what's coming and can hit the ground running."

Lesson #4: We were mixing apples and oranges

Another traditional practice, says Greg, was that the department would often combine water main work with surface work. "We were asking companies to create a soup-to-nuts bid where they had to redo the water main, resurface the road, and build new curbs and sidewalks."

When the team look at the data, they learned that these combined projects led to higher overall costs. "It seems logical once you start to think about it," comments Greg. "The contractors that do underground work don't do surface work, and vice versa. So if a project had a mix, we'd have one contractor as the prime and subcontract out the other half—which meant we were paying a premium."

The team found that they could get lower overall costs if they bid the underground work first, got that work done, and *then* bid the surface work.

Solution & Results

The combination of the outside experts' input and additional data analysis of previous contracts led the team to come up with the following list of recommendations:

- Bid all projects with construction method choice (open cut or bored) and award on lowest cost solution
- Bid larger (total footage) main replacement projects by replacing all underperforming water mains in an entire neighborhood (as opposed to individual streets)
- Bid the larger neighborhood replacement projects in the cold weather months (December to March)
- Bid the larger neighborhood replacement projects with a minimal amount of additional construction work not directly associated with the water main replacement work (don't add lots of surface paving work into the replacement project)

In brief, the team expected that asking for bids for large (>3,000 feet), stand-alone main replacement work in the cold weather months will produce lowest unit costs.

Results

"These changes dramatically reduced our water main cost structure," says Greg. "As a matter of fact, the very first project we bid after all this came together was very large—15,000 feet—with no surface work, and plastic pipe that was bored. The cost per foot was $43. That was down from $60 or more per foot." (See Figure 37, next page.)

Figure 37: BEFORE and AFTER bids (cost per foot)

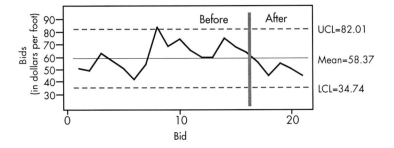

Prior to this project, there was a lot of variability in bids for laying water mains and the cost-per-foot was drifting above $60. As a result of this project, the cost-per-foot has moved much closer to $40 and there is less variability.

The lower costs have allowed the city to meet (or at least come close to) the goal of replacing six miles of water mains per year. (See Figure 38.)

Figure 38:
Miles of Water Mains Replaced

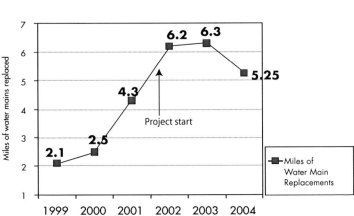

Together, the savings and lowered cost-per-foot of replacing water mains let the city achieve its goal within budget, work that would have cost about $300,000 more under the old system.

What Made This Work

- **Having everyone in the room together, and especially including contractors in our discussions.** Without a doubt, the biggest breakthroughs in this project came from listening to external experts (our contractors). They opened the eyes of team members to preconceived notions that may have once been true but weren't any longer.

- **Verifying suppositions with data.** For years, the city had acted under certain suppositions about what would make for the least expensive way to replace water mains. Once we started talking to contractors, however, we learned that these suppositions were likely wrong. Having new opinions added into the mix was very enlightening, but the team took the extra step this time around of verifying the new options with data.

- **Acting quickly.** This sounds like a contradiction to the notion that we verified opinions with data, but in fact it is a sign of Six Sigma expertise to know when it's OK to act without further analysis and when data is needed. In our case, there were some obvious changes that jumped out in the first weeks of the project—such as allowing the bidding vendors to choose their own method for laying the pipes. As a general rule, it is best to verify problems with data before taking action, but here, the proposed procedural changes had only a upside and no potential downside, so they were implemented immediately.

"It was a good experience to see the data prove out some of the things we already wanted to do and discount some other things that at the time seemed to make sense to us."

Matthew Wirtz

CHAPTER 7

Getting Started

The gains we've seen in Fort Wayne from our decision to strive for business excellence have been so profound that we can't imagine a city *not* wanting to get involved in Lean and Six Sigma. But it takes serious thought and commitment because the changes don't come easily.

Where to start? A detailed plan is beyond the scope of this book, but my colleagues and I have put together some tips to help you get started:

1. Network
2. Beg, borrow, buy, build (in that order)
3. Use your convening authority
4. Be a learner
5. Walk the talk
6. A good beginning makes a good ending
7. Find your leaders

Tip 1: Network

Here's a challenge for you. Call up the CEOs of the top 5 or 10 employers in your area and ask if they are using Lean Six Sigma (or an improvement method like it with a different name). The terms Lean and Six Sigma may not be recognized at all within many city governments, but they *are* well known in the business world. The odds are good that at least several and perhaps even the majority will answer yes. Then ask if you and your department heads can visit for half a day to see what they're doing with Lean Six Sigma.

Most major companies and thousands of smaller companies in the U.S. are using Lean Six Sigma, so the odds are in your favor that you'll have local examples of Lean Six Sigma in action. This is especially true if you have local operations or affiliates of companies such as ITT, Raytheon, GE, Lockheed Martin, Bank of America, Xerox, and many others. There may also be local business organizations (such as our TQM Network) or chapters of national organizations (such as the American Society for Quality) that have resources that you can tap.

Piggybacking on the efforts of private companies and professional organizations not only provides you with opportunities for learning and inspiration, but also allows these other organizations to take pride in helping make your city a better place to work and live.

While you're at this networking business, think beyond your county borders. We're hoping that a lot of cities will follow our example and begin using Lean Six Sigma business practices, so there may be a number of your peers who are going through the same challenges. Help start a support group of these peers or a sharing website so you can learn from what others are doing, and vice versa.

The High Performance Government Network

The success of Six Sigma and Lean in Fort Wayne has generated interest both locally and around the world. To help other municipalities get involved, we are now partnering with the Indiana State Chamber of Commerce, Indiana University School of Public and Environmental Affairs, the Indiana Association of Cities and Towns (IACT), and others to develop a new association we're calling the **High Performance Government Network** (www.hpgnetwork.com).

HPG Network is a not-for-profit, membership-based learning network designed for chief elected officials (such as mayors and town managers) It includes:

• highly focused, intensive, peer-based learning and coaching

• high-performance partnerships where mayors and business leaders interested in helping their cities improve will work together to share lessons and resources

• a clearinghouse for learning and consulting resources to give mayors proven tools, facts, and leadership skills necessary to implement improvement efforts

• a powerful broadband video learning and communication connectivity to provide real-time interactivity and rich media experiences

• a common, metrics-driven process of high-performance government improvement

Tip 2: Beg, borrow, buy, build (in that order)

When it comes to getting things accomplished that are outside the norm of city government, my mantra is to work through the four Bs in order:

- **Beg:** Ask local businesses and professional organizations if you can piggyback onto existing training courses. (It's quite easy to frame this as a civic responsibility!) They may let you send one or two people to their courses for free (as ITT did for us) or charge discounted prices (which was our arrangement with the TQM Network).

- **Borrow:** If begging doesn't work, ask if you can borrow resources. Large companies in particular may have Black Belts or Master Black Belts they could loan to you periodically to help guide your teams and/or develop and deliver training. If they can't lend you staff, they may have existing training curricula or other resources they would be willing to lend to you.

- **Buy:** If the first two options don't work, look around for packaged training programs that you could purchase or send your staff to, perhaps through a local technical college or quality network. You can also hire an external consultant (sometimes called an implementation partner) to develop and deliver training to your staff. See below for more details on these options.

- **Build**: If all else fails, the last resort is to build your own training program from scratch. This can be very time consuming, and if not done by people who are knowledgeable in Six Sigma, wouldn't serve your purposes, anyway—so you'd be better off going back to one of the first three options!

And don't forget to check local universities and community or technical colleges. In many states, the technical colleges have become *the* place for small companies to get training in quality improvement. Why shouldn't a city government take advantage of the same resources?

Building credibility

Need another reason to make connections with private sector companies in your area who are using Lean and Six Sigma? Greg Meszaros gives a good one:

"Every six months or so, Graham would conduct these CEO roundtables where other CEOs would come to talk about Six Sigma. And that's where I started to think, 'Raytheon is using this. Parkview Hospital systems. ITT. This isn't just some cockamamie idea of the mayor's.' I had never heard of Six Sigma until the mayor brought it in. I would have just thought it was something he invented. But as you started to see that the best industries were using this, you knew it was for real."

Tip 3: Use your convening authority

There's one thing that the heads of government agencies can do better than almost anyone else: bring talent and resources to the table—the power to "convene." I'm always amazed at how much gets accomplished when you bring together people who normally either don't cross paths or are on opposite sides of an issue. A mayor can say to just about anybody in the city, "Will you come to a meeting to try to deal with this problem?" People may not help, they may say they don't want to do it. But rarely do they turn down the convening authority request of the mayor.

That convening power is one reason we've been able to use our B.E.S.T. teams so effectively. B.E.S.T. (Building Excellent Services with Teams) originally referred to one of the broad goals I set at the start of my first term (see p. 5), but now we use that term in reference to a special kind of diverse team brought together to tackle citywide issues. (See sidebar, next page.)

Tip 4: Be a learner

I once read a quote that was something like "90% of what every CEO needs to know to be successful is not something in their field of discipline or interest." If you're going to be a leader of the future, you have to get out of your silo of knowledge and find out what you don't know. I had the luxury of having an extensive background with quality improvement, Lean, and Six Sigma. You don't have to be

Using B.E.S.T. to tackle broad issues

By their nature, our Six Sigma and Lean teams are limited to attacking problems contained within a single process or department. But we have urgent issues confronting the city, and for those we developed the B.E.S.T. team concept.

You may recall from p. 5 that B.E.S.T. (Building Excellent Services with Teams) originally referred to one of the three strategic goals established in my first term. Now, it refers to teams comprising both public and private sector representatives who tackle citywide challenges.

Our county Board of Health originally was unprepared to tackle the West Nile virus, which appeared quite suddenly. They kept to their traditional spraying plans, which were not particularly environmentally friendly nor preventative. A B.E.S.T. team of community leaders investigated West Nile and came up with a new plan. The team discovered it was far better to attack the larval stages of the mosquito in standing water (a path that was far less toxic than spraying). They also developed health guidelines for the community. We printed 200,000 pieces of literature and put in motion plans to eliminate standing water throughout the community.

We've had other B.E.S.T. teams tackle citywide safety problems, evaluate our public information functions, address risk management in the city, improve communication with the Hispanic community, and so on.

Though data plays a role in these teams, the requirements are less strict than for our Six Sigma and Lean teams. And unlike the latter, the B.E.S.T. teams usually conclude with recommendations to be implemented by others (city agencies and community groups).

an expert in these fields to do it yourself. You *do* need a basic understanding, however, of the core principles. Usually a two-day overview (Executive Leader or "Champion training" in Six Sigma parlance) is enough to make a good start. The TQM Network (www.tqmnet.com) offers an excellent two-day executive overview.

Tip 5: Walk the talk

If you are a mayor or the head of a city department, you have to be fully involved in Lean Six Sigma or you can't expect others to be. If you're not willing to change, others won't. If you don't practice data-driven thinking and decision making, if you're not willing to use proven business practices, then no one else will either.

You don't need to become a Black Belt yourself, familiar with the intricacies of data collection and analysis, but the *mindset* of Lean Six Sigma should imbue your management style. As discussed several times already, walking the talk for me is most evident in my favorite questions to ask of city employees:

- Who are your customers?
- Are we doing better? How do we measure that?
- What data do you have supporting this idea?

I also drop in on the Green Belt and Black Belt training sessions to meet the people who will shape our future success. I attend and listen to *all* final reports from training participants.

City staff like Zenovia Pearson (above) and Kathy Sunday (right) never know when I may drop in to ask my "favorite questions" about data, customers, and measuring progress.

As much as possible within the scope of your influence, try to get a similar involvement from others in your government. The more that people touch, feel, and see the efforts directly, the better they will understand the power of Lean Six Sigma and how to use it to their advantage.

Tip 6: A good beginning makes a good ending

You need to treat Lean and Six Sigma as you would any major strategic effort. Write your own high-performance business plan showing investments over at least a 24-month horizon (that's long enough not to feel too rushed, but short enough to produce visible, measurable results fairly quickly to share internally and with the public). Make sure that department goals are aligned with your overall strategic goals.

As part of that planning, pull out all the stops in making sure that your first training sessions will go well. If you treat the training cavalierly, so will everyone else. If you make sure you get the best trainers available and give people a positive training experience (and good project results to go along with it), everyone will see that you are serious.

In government, where administrations come and go, it's natural that a number of employees will have the attitude of "He won't last through the next election!" Gaining early successes is part of the strategy for making sure that attitude is never accepted as the norm. That's in part why the choice of the initial Champions, Black Belt and Green Belt candidates, and projects is so critical. Our all-volunteer approach worked well because it helped ensure that the first participants were motivated to learn and apply the new methods.

For our first projects, we chose highly visible problems, like filling potholes and making key customer-impact processes faster and easier for the customer. People notice when there's a pothole on their street that's filled in hour, not days. Builder and developers notice when they can get complete projects approved in days instead of months.

Tip 7: Find the Leaders

One of the early turning points in our Six Sigma effort was when Ted Rhinehart, who was then the Director of City Utilities and Public Works, got it. He told me, "I see it. I understand it. I understand you want it."

Ted had a background of innovation, a willingness to try new things. He really worked to drive change in the utilities area and public works, which accomplished several things:

- He became a strong advocate for Six Sigma, able to speak with confidence to his peers and employees.
- His leadership is why we had early successes we could use as examples, which not only helped convince others what was possible but provided a counter-argument to complaints such as "Do I really have to do all this data collection? This might take me six months. I'm too busy."

The more you can do to find and encourage leaders like Ted (and now Greg Meszaros and Bob Kennedy) at all levels of your organization, the more quickly your Six Sigma efforts will take root and spread.

Conclusion

The main message I want you to take away from this chapter is that everything you need to get started is either in your city or not far away. Six Sigma and Lean are both being used by vast numbers of companies in this country, and some of them will be on your doorstep. Go visit them, set up an assessment team that pairs their experts with your staff to evaluate what's needed in your city. Put a plan in place. And act.

As I hope you can tell from this chapter, and really from the book as a whole, we did not do everything perfectly when deploying Six Sigma and Lean. I hope you'll find that encouraging, knowing that you can generate great results even without being perfect. I hope you'll learn from our experience and do an even better than job we did.

What we had going for us was my conviction, which preceded my administration, to apply the best business practices I could find to government. We also had the dedication and hard work of more people than I can name. I'm confident that most city employees are going to be like those in Fort Wayne: eager to learn and willing to work hard to make change a reality. So the real key is having leaders who are committed to making this happen. If you have that, the possibilities are endless.

Epilogue

A hundred years ago, it was much easier being a city. All you had to do was provide a few basic services. Collect taxes. Lay down a few sewers. Hire police officers. Build a few schools. Kids played pick-up games in the streets or on unused lots. Businesses sought you out likely because of some unique resource you had: ports, rivers, railways, lumber.

No one was demanding that the city build trails or playgrounds. Businesses weren't considering taking their jobs overseas. Builders were eager to put up houses.

Now, the list of things that cities must do well is staggering. We must be able to fill potholes quickly. Purify water. Issue permits. Fight fires. Respond to terrorist threats. Fix streetlights. Answer customer inquiries. Collect trash. Enforce laws. Pave streets. Mow parks. Promote the city to prospective citizens and employers. Attract investment. Build bike paths. Preserve the peace. Provide any reporter or citizen with a record of any phone call or meeting, or copies of financial information. Create a vibrant downtown. Follow federal mandates. Implement laws and regulations.

Further, we must do all this while being audited and monitored by state and federal government bureaucracies—not to mention being mandated to provide services without funding—all to limits beyond the imagining of our private-sector counterparts.

Unlike a private company, we can't exit these businesses no matter what challenges they impose on cities. We are expected to provide the full range of services. And in today's world, we must do all of this exceptionally well to compete for jobs in a global economy.

Our achievements with Lean and Six Sigma are contributing to this ability to compete at a high-performance level. Better still, the new skills and competencies gained by our city employees are helping to create the confidence that we can develop innovative ways to make measurable progress on long-entrenched problems and challenges. We are using our skills in collaborative problem solving to bring together the public and private sector leaders to look at ways we can create a safer city, have a better-educated workforce, maximize our technological capabilities, and make sure our children have the skills they need to thrive in the modern world.

Here are just three examples of high-performance public/private partnerships that are helping us build a better city:

1. High Speed Broadband for All (aka Fiber Optics to the Home)

Our goal is to make Fort Wayne a leader in high-speed broadband technology infrastructure and killer applications. Fort Wayne provides high-speed broadband to more than 128,000 households by partnering with Verizon on its fiber-to-the-premises technology. This network makes Fort Wayne one of the most desirable cities in the country for broadband for residents and businesses.

New high-speed broadband cables are being laid down throughout Fort Wayne. Photo courtesy of Verizon, which has been a strong partner in making this goal a reality for our community.

Fort Wayne is the first community in Indiana to link all schools with high-speed broadband. We have 90 schools, 3,000 teachers and 54,000 students that benefit for this technology through the Ace Link Broadband Network. High-speed broadband applications include teacher training, distance learning and virtual town hall meetings.

Through our Innovation Initiative, we are creating new services via groups we call iTeams (i for innovation). The Net Literacy iTeam, for example, is increasing computer access and Internet literacy to underserved youth, families and senior citizens.

Health professionals and the Virtual Medicine Eye iTeam are working to provide real-time remote diagnosis for diabetic patients with possible retinal problems by using a retinal camera. High-speed broadband connection to a digital camera allows for retinal images to be reviewed by doctors at another location, providing fast, precise diagnosis of eye problems. The information is then filed electronically to be used for future patient check-ups and treatment.

In partnership with local company, Indiana Data Center, Fort Wayne has become a leader in providing WiFi services. A mesh WiFi system was launched in 2002. It now provides citywide service with free services downtown at libraries, hospitals, schools, as well as at the airport.

WiFi hotspots also enhance public safety. Fort Wayne Police Department officers can file their shift reports without ever leaving their district. That means more police on the street and less crime in our neighborhoods.

2. Renaissance Pointe

Hanna-Creighton
Neighborhood Revitalization

Hanna Creighton is the story of the typical urban neighborhood of our era:

- In the early decades of the 1900s, it was a thriving neighborhood, teeming with families and neighborhood amenities and services.

- During the 1960s and beyond, families started to leave the neighborhood in search of a different lifestyle. Over time, amenities and services declined.

- The neighborhood slowly deteriorated and eventually more than 400 abandoned buildings were demolished.

By 1990, with high levels of vacancy and low levels of home-ownership, Hanna-Creighton had become one of the poorest census tracts in the state of Indiana. To make things worse, in 1997 this once-thriving neighborhood near the former Bowser Pump Company building was the site of a million tires burning in an abandoned factory.

For some neighborhoods this is where the story ends. For Hanna-Creighton it is where a new story would begin. Today the neighborhood (now called Renaissance Pointe) is an exciting public-private partnership with new buildings and investment to prove it.

Shortly after the tire fire, the City began working with the neighborhood on a plan to rebuild the area. A new 50-unit senior housing rental development called Phoenix Manor opened in 2002. In 2003 at the cost of more than $8 million, we added a campus at the intersection of Hanna and Creighton that includes three new public buildings: a new branch of the county library system, new headquarters for the Fort Wayne Urban League, and a new facility for Head Start. Several area churches, schools, and other organizations have also improved their facilities, further strengthening the neighborhood.

In 2005, the City took the neighborhood's vision of a home-ownership community to an entirely new level when it launched a home-ownership initiative to bring back the traditional front porch community in Hanna-Creighton. The master development plan calls for architecturally significant homes built with alley-serviced detached garages, old fashioned tree-lined streets and lighting. An urban trail will run through the center of the development. There are also commercial, retail, and mixed-use spaces. The local YMCA was inspired by this initiative to build a new $9 million YMCA on the former site of the tire fire, where the urban trail terminates.

Hanna-Creighton then...

Too little investment in the neighborhood meant there were a lot of run-down houses and abandoned sites. A huge pile of abandoned tires once caught fire as well.

... and Now

A new complex near the old "tire fire" site houses the new

Urban League headquarters, a public library, and a Head Start facility. New housing is going up and old houses are being renovated.

3. Regional Public Safety Academy

If 9/11 and Katrina taught us anything, it was that improving communication and cooperation between the various first responders involved in emergencies and disasters was an imperative, not a luxury. In July 2006, Fort Wayne began building a regional public safety academy on the site of an abandoned mall. The facility will provide police, fire, emergency medical services, and homeland security training and education for professionals and students from the Northeast Indiana region.

Making this academy a reality required a new level of cooperation across city, county, state, and federal agencies. A new high-performance partnership will provide training and education that is just as state-of-the-art as the new facility.

Highlights of the Regional Public Safety Academy

What: One of the first cross-functional public safety training centers in the country.

Target Users: Police, fire, emergency medical services, homeland security, public safety professionals and volunteers

Size: 132,000 square feet

Facilities: Conference areas, a planning center, state-of-the-art live firing range, firearms training simulator, wet and dry fire training rooms, large indoor shooting range,

An abandoned mall...

...is torn down...

and becomes a thriving retail center while construction continues on the Public Safety Academy

health and fitness center, emergency vehicle driving simulator, and customized exercise scenario software. (State-of-the-art fiber optics broadband will also enable delivery of training to all Allen County schools.)

Activities: On-site and distance learning, high school through adult education in the form of Fire and Police Training Academies; emergency medical training, homeland security and anti-terrorism training. Citizens and businesses leaders will be trained for community preparedness. Special youth learning programs will encourage participation in the Safe City initiative. The Academy will be available to serve as a satellite location for the Indiana Department of Homeland Security Division of Preparedness & Training, the Indiana Law Enforcement Academy, the Indiana State Fire Academy, the Department of Health and other state or federal agencies.

Support partnership: Ivy Tech State College, the Regional Anthis Career Center, the Indiana National Guard, Indiana-Purdue University at Fort Wayne, Indiana Tech, Tri-State, St Francis and Taylor Universities are collaborating to provide the education, training, and public-safety related college degrees.

Index